Integrated Chinese

中文聽說讀寫

Traditional Character Edition
Textbook

Tao-chung Yao and Yuehua Liu
Liangyan Ge, Yea-fen Chen, Nyan-ping Bi and Xiaojun Wang

Cheng & Tsui Company

First edition 1997
2002 Printing

Cheng & Tsui Company
25 West Street
Boston, MA 02111-1213 USA

Library of Congress Catalog Card Number: 97-068898

Traditional Character Edition
ISBN 0-88727-262-2

Companion workbooks, character workbooks and audio tapes are also available from the publisher.

Printed in the United States of America

PUBLISHER'S NOTE

The Cheng & Tsui Company is pleased to announce the most recent addition to its Asian Language Series, *Integrated Chinese*. This entirely new course program for the beginning to advanced student of Mandarin Chinese will incorporate textbooks, workbooks, character workbooks, teacher's manual, audio tapes, and in the near future, video tapes, CD-ROM computer programs and interactive multimedia programs. Field-tested since 1994, this series has been very well received. It is our intention to keep it a dynamic product by continuing to add, revise and refine the content as we get your valuable feedback.

This series seeks to train students in all four language skills: listening, speaking, reading and writing. It utilizes a variety of pedagogical approaches—grammar translation, audio-lingual, direct method, total physical response—to achieve the desired results. Because no two Chinese language programs are the same, *Integrated Chinese* provides those classes that cover the lessons more speedily with additional material in the form of Supplementary Vocabulary. The Supplementary Vocabulary section, however, is purely optional.

The *C&T Asian Language Series* is designed to publish and widely distribute quality language texts as they are completed by such leading institutions as the Beijing Language Institute, as well as other significant works in the field of Asian languages developed in the United States and elsewhere.

We welcome readers' comments and suggestions concerning the publications in this series. Please contact the following members of the Editorial Board:

Professor Shou-hsin Teng, Chief Editor
3 Coach Lane, Amherst, MA 01002

Professor Dana Scott Bourgerie
Asian and Near Eastern Languages, Brigham Young University, Provo, UT 84602

Professor Samuel Cheung
Dept. of Oriental Languages, University of California, Berkeley, CA 94720

Professor Ying-che Li
Dept. of East Asian Languages, University of Hawaii, Honolulu, HI 96822

Professor Timothy Light
Office of the Provost, Western Michigan University, Kalamazoo, MI 49008

Preface

How Did It Get Started?

Integrated Chinese (IC) originated as a set of teaching materials designed to suit the needs of the curriculum of the Chinese School of the East Asian Summer Language Institute (EASLI) at Indiana University. The overall planning was done in the summer of 1993 at the weekly Chinese School faculty meetings. A couple of sample lessons were also designed during that summer. Seven of the Chinese School teachers, Nyan-ping Bi (MIT), Yea-fen Chen (University of Wisconsin-Wilwaukee), Liangyan Ge (University of Notre Dame), Yuehua Liu (Harvard University), Yaohua Shi (University of Massachusetts at Amherst), Xiaojun Wang (Western Michigan University), Tao-chung (Ted) Yao (University of Hawaii), participated in this project and started to work on it in the fall.

During the fall of 1993, the first ten lessons of both Level One and Two were written and distributed to all seven members of the textbook committee for their comments and suggestions. During the Christmas holidays, all seven worked for ten days in South Hadley, Massachusetts and revised the first ten lessons of the first two levels, and wrote ten more lessons for each level. They continued to work on this project in their spare time, throughout the spring of 1994 and joined forces again in Bloomington, Indiana three weeks before the beginning of EASLI to finalize the first draft of this new set of materials. It was field tested at the Chinese School in the summer of 1994.

Both Level One and Level Two Chinese courses at the EASLI Chinese School used the materials, with positive results. The student consensus was that they had learned a lot in just nine weeks. This initial success prompted the decision to improve IC further for use in regular year-long programs, as well. During the 1994-1995 academic year, IC was field-tested at a half dozen schools in the United States. After receiving some feedback from the users, IC was revised in the summer of 1996. Some seventeen universities and colleges field tested the 1996 version of IC.

Why Use the Name Integrated Chinese?

We came up with the title *Integrated Chinese* because it reflects what we intend to accomplish. We place emphasis on all four skills (listening, speaking, reading and writing) and incorporate into our teaching materials those teaching philosophies and methods which might help our students to master the Chinese language. Furthermore, we utilize any modern technology that might aid the process of language instruction. The scheme of integration is further elaborated below.

All Four Language Skills Are Stressed

The Chinese title of *Integrated Chinese*, which is simply "中文聽説讀寫"
(Zhōngwén: Tīng, Shuō, Dú, Xiě), reflects our belief that a healthy language program should be a well-balanced one, paying attention to all four skills, listening, speaking, reading and writing. To ensure that students will be strong in all skills, and because we believe that each of the four skills needs special training, the exercises in the workbook are divided into four sections of listening, speaking, reading and writing. Within each section, there are two types of exercises, namely, traditional exercises (such as fill-in-the- blank, sentence completion, translation, etc.) to help students build a solid foundation, and communication-oriented exercises to prepare students to face the real world.

Basic Organizational Principles

In recent years, a very important fact has been recognized by the field of language teaching: the ultimate goal of learning a language is to communicate in that language. As a result, many communication-oriented language textbooks have been produced. However, the Chinese language field has produced very few communication-oriented textbooks, and they cannot satisfy the need of a full-fledged program which offers beginning through advanced Chinese language courses. Our field is in desperate need for a set of Chinese language instructional materials that is communication-oriented, yet carefully graded to provide students with a solid foundation in grammar. In other words, our field needs a set of materials which will give students grammatical tools and also prepare them to function in a Chinese language environment. The materials should cover all levels of instruction (from beginning to advanced and beyond), with smooth transitions from one level to the next. The materials should first cover everyday life topics and gradually move to more abstract subject matters. The materials should not be limited to one method or one approach but should use any teaching method and approach that can produce good results. Following are some of the features of *Integrated Chinese* which make it different from other currently available Chinese language textbooks.

- *Integrating Pedagogical and Authentic Materials*

All of the materials are graded in *Integrated Chinese*. We believe that students can grasp the materials better if they learn simple and easy to control language items before the more difficult or complicated ones. We also believe that our students should be taught some authentic materials even in the first year of language instruction. Therefore, most of the pedagogical materials are actually simulated authentic materials. Real authentic materials (written by native Chinese speakers for native Chinese speakers) are incorporated in the lessons when appropriate.

• *Integrating Written Style and Spoken Style*

One way to measure a person's Chinese proficiency is to see if s/he can handle the "written style" (書面語, shūmiànyǔ) with ease. The "written style" language is more formal and literal than the "spoken style" (口語, kǒuyǔ); however, it is also widely used in news broadcasts and formal speeches. In addition to the "spoken style" Chinese, basic "written style" expressions are gradually introduced in *Integrated Chinese* .

• *Integrating Traditional and Simplified Characters*

We believe that students should learn to handle Chinese language materials in both the traditional and the simplified forms. However, we also realize that it could be rather confusing and overwhelming if we teach our students both the traditional and the simplified forms from day one. A reasonable solution to this problem is for the student to concentrate on one form, either traditional or simplified, at the first level, and to acquire the other form during the second level. Therefore, for level one, we have prepared two sets of materials, one using traditional characters and one using simplified characters, to meet different needs. To accommodate those who wish to learn both traditional and simplified forms at the same time, we have included simplified-character texts in the appendices of the traditional-character version, and traditional-character texts in the appendices of the simplified-characters version. The users will also find that both forms of characters are used in the vocabulary index at the end of the textbook. There are also two versions of the workbook and the character workbook for level one. In the traditional-character version of the Character Workbook, simplified characters are provided, and in the simplified-character version of the Character Workbook, traditional characters are also provided.

We believe that by the second year of studying Chinese, all students should be taught to read both traditional and simplified characters. Therefore, the text of each lesson is shown in both traditional and simplified forms, and the vocabulary list in each lesson also contains both forms. Considering that students in a second-year Chinese language class might come from different backgrounds and that some of them might have learned the traditional form and some others the simplified form, students should be allowed to write in either traditional or simplified forms. It is important to make the student write in one form only, and not a hybrid of both forms.

• *Integrated Teaching Approach*

Realizing that there is no one single teaching method which is adequate in training a student to be proficient in all four language skills, we employ a variety of teaching methods and approaches to maximize the teaching results. In addition to the communicative approach, we also use other methods such as grammar-translation, audio-lingual, direct method, total physical response, etc.

- *Modern Technology*

Integrated Chinese is intended to be a set of instructional materials which will include textbooks, workbooks, character workbooks, teaching aids, audio tapes, videotapes, CD-ROM, laser discs, computer programs, and interactive multimedia programs. We have already established a homepage (http://nts.lll.hawaii.edu/tedyao/ICUsers/) on the World Wide Web which will serve as a resource center as well as a support group for the users. New materials (such as new exercises or teaching activities developed by the original IC textbook committee, or by others) will be shared, and teaching ideas will be exchanged on the Internet. Students can do some of the exercises on the internet, and teachers can check the answers.

The Designing of Integrated Chinese

Currently, the *Integrated Chinese* series contains the following volumes:

Level One
Textbook, Part I (Traditional-character version)
Textbook, Part II (Traditional-character version)
Workbook, Part I (Traditional-character version)
Workbook, Part II (Traditional-character version)
Character Workbook, Part I (Traditional-character version)
Character Workbook, Part II (Traditional-character version)
Textbook, Part I (Simplified-character version)
Textbook, Part II (Simplified-character version)
Workbook, Part I (Simplified-character version)
Workbook, Part II (Simplified-character version)
Character Workbook, Part I (Simplified-character version)
Character Workbook, Part II (Simplified-character version)
Teacher's Manual

Level Two
Textbook
Workbook
Teacher's Manual

We did not prepare a character workbook for level two because, by the second year, students should have a good sense of how Chinese characters are composed, eliminating the need for such a book. The teacher's manuals are, as the title suggests, for the teachers to use. Currently, they are basically answer keys. However, we will add classroom activities to the manuals in the 1998 edition. Although there are only two levels of IC at this moment, we do intend to prepare levels three and four in the near future.

About the Format

Please note that the formats of Part I and Part II of the Level I Textbook are somewhat different. To make it easier for students to read the Chinese characters, we use a size 18 Chinese font for the main texts and a size 16 Chinese font for the grammar and drill sections. In the authentic reading materials, such as newspapers and magazines, the Chinese characters are usually rather small. To train students to get used to smaller print, we decided to reduce the Chinese font to size 14. Considering that many teachers might want to teach their students how to speak the language before teaching them how to read Chinese characters, we decided to place the *pinyin* text before the Chinese-character text in each of the eleven lessons in Part I of the Level I Textbook. For the same reason, all Chinese sentences in the grammar and drill sections are preceded by their *pinyin* counterparts.

Since *pinyin* is only a vehicle to help students to learn the pronunciation of the Chinese language and it is not a replacement of the Chinese writing system, it is important that our students can read out loud in Chinese by looking at the Chinese text and not just the *pinyin* text. To train students to deal with the Chinese text directly and not to rely on *pinyin*, we moved the *pinyin* text to the end of each lesson in Part II of the Level I Textbook. Students can refer to the *pinyin* text to verify a sound when necessary. For the grammar and the drill sections, we simply eliminated the *pinyin* text altogether, thus ensuring that students will deal only with Chinese characters.

We are fully aware of the fact that no two Chinese language programs are identical and that each program has its own requirements. Some schools will cover a lot of material in one year while some others will cover considerably less. Trying to meet the needs of as many schools as possible, we decided to cover a wide range of materials, both in terms of vocabulary and grammar, in *Integrated Chinese*. To facilitate oral practice and to allow students to communicate in real-life situations, many supplementary vocabulary items are added to each lesson. However, the characters in the supplementary vocabulary sections are not included in the Character Workbook. In the Character Workbook, each of the characters is given a frequency indicator based on the Hànyǔ Pínlǜ Dà Cídiǎn (漢語頻率大辭典). Teachers can decide for themselves which characters must be learned.

Different types of notes provide explanations for selected expressions in the text. In the dialogues, expressions followed by a superscript numeral are explained in notes directly below the text; expressions followed by a superscript "G" plus a numeral are explained in grammar notes in the grammar section of the lesson.

Future Plans

We are firmly committed to providing our field with a high-quality Chinese language text series which will suit the needs of most, if not all, Chinese language teachers and students. To that end, we intend periodically to update the content and the format of IC to ensure that it reflects the most current Chinese language in use, and the most effective approaches in language pedagogy.

This 1997 edition of IC is an initial edition. Our plan is to publish a revised version with more illustrations and authentic materials in the near future. If you notice any typos or other problems in the current version, please help us improve this series by contacting the Publisher or us at:

Ted Yao
Dept. of East Asian Languages and Literatures
388 Moore Hall
1890 East West Road
University of Hawaii at Manoa
Honolulu, HI 96822

Email: tyao@hawaii.edu
Phone: 808-956-2071
Fax: 808-956-9515

tcy (Honolulu, HI)
yhl (Boston, MA)

TABLE OF CONTENTS

ACKNOWLEDGMENTS

The project of compiling a series of new Chinese language teaching materials was initiated in the summer of 1993 at the East Asian Summer Language Institute (EASLI) at Indiana University. The first draft of *Integrated Chinese* took about eight months to complete. It was truly a collaborative effort, with two teams of teachers simultaneously working on two sets of textbooks, student workbooks and teacher's manuals. Some of our colleagues contributed to both sets of materials. Professor Yaohua Shi, a member of our *Integrated Chinese, Level Two* team, prepared the draft of the *Introduction* and wrote a good number of cultural notes to the texts presented here, among other valuable contributions to the *Integrated Chinese, Level One* volumes.

Since the inception of *Integrated Chinese*, teachers and students at many institutions have offered us extremely helpful comments and suggestions. The entire series was adopted on a trial basis at the EASLI Chinese School in the summer of 1994. In the fall of 1994, our colleagues at the University of Massachusetts at Amherst, Amherst College and Mount Holyoke College graciously offered to field test *Integrated Chinese*. We are indebted to Hua Lan, Mi-mi Liu, Xiaoping Teng and Alvin Cohen for reading the earlier drafts and offering us invaluable comments and suggestions. We would also like to thank Shou-hsin Teng for his advice and technical support. Subsequently, *Integrated Chinese* was adopted at more than twenty universities and colleges around the country, including Washington University in St. Louis, University of Wisconsin at Madison, San Diego State University, University of Iowa and University of Notre Dame. Our gratitude goes to Professors Alice Cheang, Baochang He, Chuanren Ke, Fengtao Wu, Hongming Zhang and Zhengsheng Zhang for their vote of confidence and helpful feedback.

At EASLI, Mr. Zhijie Jia, Ms. Jing Shen and Ms. Aihua Guo were generous with their time and expertise. Ms. Rebecca Hunt, Ms. Margot Lenhart and Ms. Karen McCabe fine-tuned the English in the volumes. Katy Yao and Deborah Struemph helped us type and photocopy the earlier drafts. To all of them, we would like to extend our heartfelt thanks. Thanks are also due to James Landers, Jung-ying lu-Chen, Susan Zeng and Shu-fen Fujitani for reading the drafts and making invaluable suggestions and to Heidi Wong for editing portions of the current version. We are indebted to Jeffrey Hayden for preparing the *Character Workbook* and Indices. Jeffrey also painstakingly proofread the manuscripts and made useful comments and suggestions.

We are most grateful to the resident artist of the University of Hawaii, Peter Kobayashi, for preparing the illustrations for the teachers to use in the classrooms, and for allowing us to include some of the illustrations in the current version. We must, of course, also thank our contracted artist, Mr. Jian Xu, for providing us with the illustrations which highlight the theme of each lesson in the *Integrated Chinese, Level One* textbook.

Several surveys have been conducted in past years to solicit comments and suggestions on *Integrated Chinese*. We would like to express our sincere appreciation to those who participated in the surveys. What we mentioned above only represents a portion of those who have helped *Integrated Chinese* in one way or another, and it is by no means an exhaustive list.

Finally, we would like to thank Ms. K. T. Yao, Professor Yongjiang Wang, Mr. Tse-Tsang Chang, Mr. Chun-yuan Huang and Ms. Yongqing Pan for their understanding and unfailing support throughout the four years of compiling and revising *Integrated Chinese*.

Abbreviations for Grammar Terms

Abbr	*Abbreviation*
Adj	*Adjective*
Adv	*Adverb*
AV	*Auxiliary Verb*
CE	*Common Expression*
Coll	*Colloquialism*
Conj	*Conjunction*
Exc	*Exclamation*
Interj	*Interjection*
M	*Measure word*
N	*Noun*
NP	*Noun Phrase*
Nu	*Numerals*
P	*Particle*
Pr	*Pronoun*
Prep	*Preposition*
Ono	*Onomatopoeic*
QP	*Question Particle*
QPr	*Question Pronoun*
T	*Time word*
V	*Verb*
VC	*Verb plus Complement*
VO	*Verb plus Object*

Introduction

I. CHINESE PRONUNCIATION

A Chinese syllable is composed of an initial and a final. Initials consist of consonants or semi-vowels; finals consist of vowels or vowels plus one of these two nasal sounds: -[n] or -[ng]. In addition to an initial and a final, there is a tone to each Chinese syllable.

A. Simple Finals:

There are six simple finals:

a, o, e, i, u, ü

When it is pronounced by itself, **a** is a central vowel. The tongue remains in a natural, relaxed position.

o is a rounded semi-high back vowel.

e is an unrounded semi-high back vowel. To produce this vowel, first pronounce **o**, then change the shape of the mouth from rounded to unrounded. At the same time open the mouth wider. This vowel is different from "**e**" in English, which is pronounced with the tongue raised slightly forward.

i is an unrounded high front vowel. The tongue is raised higher than it would be to pronounce its counterpart in English.

u is a rounded high back vowel. The tongue is raised higher than it would be to pronounce its counterpart in English.

ü is a rounded high front vowel. To produce this vowel, first pronounce **i**, then modify the shape of the mouth from unrounded to rounded.

In Chinese **i** also represents two additional special vowels. One is an alveolar front vowel, the other an alveolar back vowel.

Note: In this book, Chinese sounds are represented by *pinyin*. Although *pinyin* symbols are the same as English letters, the actual sounds which they represent can be very different from their English counterparts. Be careful to distinguish them.

B. Initials

There are twenty-one initials in Chinese.

1.	b	p	m	f
2.	d	t	n	l
3.	g	k	h	
4.	j	q	x	
5.	z	c	s	
6.	zh	ch	sh	r

B.1: b, p, m, f

b is a bilabial unaspirated plosive. Note that the Chinese b is different from its English counterpart; it is not voiced. There are no voiced plosives in Chinese.

p is a bilabial aspirated voiceless plosive. In other words, there is a strong puff of breath when the consonant is sounded.

m is a bilabial nasal sound.

f is a labio-dental fricative. To produce this sound, press the upper teeth against the lower lip, and let the breath flow out with friction.

Note: Only the simple finals a, o, i, and u and the compound finals which start with a, o, i, or u can be combined with b, p, and m; only the simple finals a, o, and u and the compound finals which start with a, o, or u can be combined with f. When these initials are combined with o, there is actually a short u sound in between. For instance, the syllable bo (b^{u}o) actually includes a very short u sound between b and o.

Practice:

B.1.a		ba	bi	bu	bo
		pa	pi	pu	po
		ma	mi	mu	mo
		fa		fu	fo
B.1.b b vs. p		ba	pa	bu	pu
		po	bo	pi	bi
B.1.c m vs. f		ma	fa	mu	fu
B.1.d b, p, m, f		bo	po	mo	fo
		fu	mu	pu	bu

B.2: d, t, n, l

When producing d, t, n, the tip of the tongue touches the upper teethridge. The tongue is raised more to the front than it would be to pronounce their English counterparts.

d is a tongue tip alveolar unaspirated plosive. It is voiceless.

t is a tongue tip alveolar aspirated stop. It is voiceless.

n is a tongue tip alveolar nasal. It is produce by placing the tip of the tongue against the ridge behind the upper teeth.

l is a tongue tip alveolar lateral. It is different from the English "l." To produce the Chinese l the tip of the tongue should touch the alveolar ridge.

Note: Only the simple finals a, i, e, and u and the compound finals which start with a, i, e, or u can be combined with d, t, n, and l; n and l can also be combined with ü and the compound finals which start with ü.

Practice:

B.2.a

da	di	du	de	
ta	ti	tu	te	
na	ni	nu	ne	nü
la	li	lu	le	lü

B.2.b d vs. t

da	ta	di	ti
du	tu	de	te

B.2.c l vs. n

lu	lü	nu	nü
lu	nu	lü	nü

B.2.d d, t, n, l

le	ne	te	de
du	tu	lu	nu

B.3: g, k, h

g is an unaspirated voiceless velar stop.

k is an aspirated voiceless velar stop.

When producing **g**, **k**, the back of the tongue is raised against the soft palate.

h is a voiceless velar fricative. When producing **h**, the back of the tongue is raised towards the soft palate. The friction is noticeable. With English counterpart, however, the friction is not noticeable.

Note: Only the simple finals **a**, **e**, and **u** and the compound finals that start with **a**, **e**, or **u** can be combined with **g**, **k**, and **h**.

Practice:

B.3.a

gu	ge	ga
ku	ke	ka
hu	he	ha

B.3.b g vs. k

gu	ku	ge	ke

B.3.c g vs. h

gu	hu	ge	he

B.3.d k vs. h

ke	he	ku	hu

B.3.e g, k, h

gu	ku	hu
he	ke	ge

B.4: j, q, x

j is an unaspirated voiceless palatal affricate. To produce this sound, first raise the front of the tongue to the hard palate and press the the tip of the tongue against the back of the lower teeth, and then loosen the tongue and let the air squeeze out through the channel thus made. It is unaspirated and the vocal cords do not vibrate.

q is an aspirated voiceless palatal affricate. It is produced in the same manner as j, but it is aspirated.

x is a voiceless palatal fricative. To produce it, first raise the front of the tongue toward (but not touching) the hard palate and then let the air squeeze out. The vocal cords do not vibrate.

Note: The finals that can be combined with j, q and x are limited to i and ü and the compound finals which start with j, q or x. When j, q and x are combined with ü or a compound final starting with ü, the umlaut in ü is omitted and the ü appears as u.

Practice:

B.4.a	ji	ju		
	qi	qu		
	xi	xu		
B.4.b j vs. q	ji	qi	ju	qu
B.4.c q vs. x	qi	xi	qu	xu
B.4.d j vs. x	ji	xi	ju	xu
B.4.e j, q, x	ji	qi	xi	
	ju	qu	xu	

B.5: z, c, s

z is an unaspirated voiceless blade-alveolar affricate.

c is an aspirated voiceless blade-alveolar affricate.

s is a voiceless blade-alveolar fricative.

The above group of sounds is pronounced with the tongue touching the back of the upper teeth.

Note: The simple finals that can be combined with z, c, s are a, e, u and the alveolar front vowel i. When one pronounces this group of sounds, the vocal chords should vibrate. To produce the alveolar front vowel i after z, c, s, prolong the z, c, s sounds.

Practice:

B.5.a	za	zu	ze	zi
	ca	cu	ce	ci
	sa	su	se	si

B.5.b s vs. z	sa	za	su	zu
	se	ze	si	zi

B.5.c z vs. c	za	ca	zi	ci
	ze	ce	zu	cu

B.5.d s vs. c	sa	ca	si	ci
	su	cu	se	ce

B.5.e z, c, s	sa	za	ca
	su	zu	cu
	se	ze	ce
	si	zi	ci
	za	cu	se
	ci	sa	zu
	su	zi	ce

B.6: zh, ch, sh, r

zh is an unaspirated voiceless blade-palatal affricate. To produce it, first turn up the tip of the tongue against the hard palate, then loosen it and let the air squeeze out the channel thus made. It is unaspirated and the vocal cords do not vibrate.

ch is an aspirated voiceless blade-palatal affricate. This sound is produced in the same manner as **zh**, but it is aspirated.

sh is a voiceless blade-palatal fricative. To produce this sound, turn up the tip of the tongue toward (but not touching) the hard palate and then let the air squeeze out. The vocal cords do not vibrate.

r is a voiced blade-palatal fricative. It is produced the same manner as **sh**, but it is voiced. The vocal cords vibrate. It is very different from the English "r."

Note: The finals that can be combined with **zh, ch, sh, r** are **a**, **e**, **u** and the alveolar back vowel **I,** as well as the compound finals which start with **a**, **e**, or **u** .

Practice:

B.6.a	zha	zhu	zhe	zhi
	cha	chu	che	chi
	sha	shu	she	shi
		ru	re	ri

B.6.b zh vs. sh	sha	zha	shu	zhu

B.6.c zh vs. ch	zha	cha	zhu	chu

B.6.d ch vs. sh	chu	shu	sha	cha

B.6.e zh, ch, sh	shi	zhi	chi	shi
	she	zhe	che	she

B.6.f sh vs. r	shu	ru	shi	ri

B.6.g r vs. l	lu	ru	li	ri

B.6.h sh, r, l	she	re	le	re

B.6.i zh, ch, r	zhe	re	che	re

B.6.j zh, ch, sh, r	sha	cha	zha	
	shu	zhu	chu	ru
	zhi	chi	shi	ri
	che	zhe	she	re

A Reference Chart for Initials

	Unaspirated stops	Aspirated stops	Nasals	Fricatives	Voiced continuants
Labials	b	p	m	f	w*
Alveolars	d	t	n		l
Dental sibilants	z	c		s	
Retroflexes	zh	ch		sh	r
Palatals	j	q		x	y*
Gutturals	g	k		h	

* See explanations of **w** and **y** in the "Spelling rules" section on p.6 below.

C. Compound Finals:

1.	āi	ēi	āo	ōu				
2.	ān	ēn	āng	ēng	ōng			
3.	īa	īao	īe	īū*	īan	īn	īang	īng	īong
4.	uā	uō	uāi	uī**	uān	ūn***	uāng	uēng	
5.	üē	üān	ǖn						
6.	ēr								

* The main vowel **o** is omitted in **iu** (iu = iou).. Therefore **iu** represents the sound **iou**. The **o** is especially conspicuous in fourth tone syllables.

** The main vowel **e** is omitted in **ui** (ui = uei). Like **iu** above, it is quite conspicuous in fourth tone syllables.

*** The main vowel **e** is omitted in **un** (un = uen).

In Chinese, compound finals are comprised of a main vowel and a secondary vowel. When the initial vowels are **a**, **e**, and **o**, they are stressed. The vowels following are soft and brief. When the initial vowels are **i**, **u**, and **ü**, the main vowels come after them. **i**, **u** and **ü** are transitional sounds. If there are vowels or nasal consonants after the main vowels, they should be unstressed as well. In a compound final, the main vowel can be affected by the phonemes before and after it. For instance, the **a** in **ian** is pronounced with a lower degree of aperture and a higher position of the tongue than the **a** in **ma**; and to pronounce the **a** in **ang** the tongue has to be positioned more to the back of the mouth than the **a** elsewhere.

In *pinyin* orthography some vowels are omitted for the sake of economy, e.g., **i(o)u**, **u(e)i**. However, when making those sounds, the vowels must not be omitted.

Spelling rules:
1. If there is no initial before **i**, **i** is a semi-vowel. In the following combinations **ia**, **ie**, **iao**, **iu**, **ian**, **iang**, **i** is written as **y**: **ya**, **ye**, **yao**, **you** (note that the **o** cannot be omitted here), **yan**, **yang**; Before **in**, **ing**, and **o**, add **y**, e.g., **yin**, **ying**, **yo**.
2. If there is no initial before **ü**, add a **y**, and drop the umlaut: **yu**, **yuan**, **yue**, **yun**.
3. **u** becomes **w** if not preceded by an initial, e.g., **wa**, **wai**, **wan**, **wang**, **wei**, **wen**, **weng**, **wo**. **u** by itself becomes **wu**.
4. **ueng** is written as **ong**, if preceded by an initial, e.g., **tong**, **dong**, **nong**, **long**.
5. In order to avoid confusion, an aspostraphe is used to separate two syllables with connecting vowels, e.g., **shi'er** and the city **Xi'an** (**xi** and **an** are two separate syllables).

Practice

C.1:   ai   ei   ao   ou

     pai   lei   dao   gou
     cai   mei   sao   shou

C.2:   an   en   ang   eng   ong

C.2.a   an vs. ang   tan   tang   chan   chang
                         zan   zhang   gan   gang

C.2.b   en vs. eng   sen   seng   shen   sheng
                         zhen   zheng   fen   feng

C.2.c   eng vs. ong   cheng chong   deng   dong
                         zheng zhong   keng   kong

C.3:   ia   iao   ie   iu   ian   in   iang   ing   iong

C.3.a   ia vs. ie   jia   jie   qia   qie
                         xia   xie   ya   ye

C.3.b   ian vs. iang   xian   xiang   qian   qiang
                         jian   jiang   yan   yang

C.3.c   in vs. ing   bin   bing   pin   ping
                         jin   jing   yin   ying

C.3.d   iu vs. iong   xiu   xiong   you   yong

C.3.e   ao vs. iao   zhao   jiao   shao   xiao
                         chao   qiao   ao   yao

C.3.f   an vs. ian   chan   qian   shan   xian
                         zhan   jian   an   yan

C.3.g   ang vs. iang   zhang jiang   shang xiang
                         chang qiang   ang   yang

C.4:   ua   uo   uai   ui   uan   un   uang

C.4.a   ua vs. uai   shua   shuai   wa   wai

C.4.b   uan vs. uang   shuan shuang chuan chuang
                         zhuan zhuang wan   wang

C.4.c	un vs. uan	dun	duan	kun	kuan
		zhun	zhuan	wen	wan

C.4.d	uo vs. ou	duo	dou	zhuo	zhou
		suo	sou	wo	ou

C.4.e	ui vs. un	tui	tun	zhui	zhun
		dui	dun	wei	wen

C.5:	üe	üan	ün

C.5.a	ün vs. un	jun	zhun	yun	wen

C.5.b	üan vs. uan	xuan	shuan	juan	zhuan
		quan	chuan	yuan	wan

C.5.c	üe	yue	que	jue

C.6:	er	ger *

* Due to the lack of words with first tone "**er**" in them, we decided to put the word "**ger**" (**ge** with **r** ending) here for the reader to get a feel for it. Please see **D.1 Practice III** below (p.11) for more examples.

D. Tones

There is a tone to every Chinese syllable.

D.1: Four tones:

There are four tones in Mandarin Chinese (i.e., 普通話 pǔtōnghuà, "common language" in mainland China; 國語 guóyǔ, "national language" in Taiwan; 華語 Huáyǔ, "the Chinese language" in Singapore and some other places): the first tone (陰平 yīnpíng), the second tone (陽平 yángpíng), the third tone (上聲 shǎngshēng), the fourth tone (去聲 qùshēng). The first tone is a high level tone with a pitch value of 55; its tone mark is " ¯ ." The second tone is a rising tone with a pitch value of 35; its tone mark is " / ." The third tone is a low tone with a pitch value of 214 (even though in reality the pitch value is more like 21) ; its tone mark is " ∨ ." The fourth tone is a falling tone with a pitch value of 51; its tone mark is " \ ."

In addition to the four tones, there also exists a neutral tone (輕聲 qīngshēng) in Mandarin Chinese. Neutral tone words include those which do not have fundamental tones (e.g., the question particle **ma**), and those which do have tones when pronounced individually, but are not stressed in certain compounds (e.g., the second **ba** in "**bàba**" or "father"). There are no tone marks for neutral tone syllables. A neutral tone syllable is pronounced briefly and softly, and its pitch value is determined by the stressed syllable immediately before it. A neutral tone following a first tone syllable, as in **māma** 媽媽, carries a pitch tone of 2. When it follows a second tone syllable, a third tone syllable, or a fourth tone syllable, its pitch value will be 3, 4, and 1 respectively.

Tones are very important in Chinese. The same syllable with different tones can have different meanings. For instance, **mā** 媽 is mother, **má** 麻 is hemp, **mǎ** 馬 is horse, **mà** 罵 is to scold, **ma** 嗎 is an interrogative particle. The four tones can be diagrammed as follows:

	First Tone	Second Tone	Third Tone	Fourth Tone

Tone marks are written above the main vowel of a syllable. The main vowel can be identified according to the following sequence: **a-o-e-i-u-ü.** For instance, in **ao** the main vowel is **a**. In **ei** the main vowel is **e**. When **i** and **u** are combined into a syllable, the tone mark is written on the second vowel: **iù, uì**.

D.1 Practice I: Monosyllabic words

1.a	Four tones	bī	bí	bǐ	bì
		pū	pú	pǔ	pù
		dà	dǎ	dá	dā
		shè	shě	shé	shē
		tí	tī	tǐ	tì
		kè	kě	kē	ké
		jǐ	jí	jì	jī
		gú	gù	gū	gǔ
1.b	1st vs. 2nd	zā	zá		
		chū	chú		
		hē	hé		
		shī	shí		
1.c	1st vs. 3rd	tū	tǔ		
		mō	mǒ		
		xī	xǐ		
		shā	shǎ		

1.d	1st vs. 4th	fā	fà
		dī	dì
		qū	qù
		kē	kè

1.e	2nd vs. 1st	hú	hū
		xí	xī
		zhé	zhē
		pó	pō

1.f	2nd vs. 3rd	gé	gě
		tí	tǐ
		jú	jǔ
		rú	rǔ

1.g	2nd vs. 4th	lú	lù
		mó	mò
		cí	cì
		zhé	zhè

1.h	3rd vs. 1st	tǎ	tā
		mǐ	mī
		gǔ	gū
		chě	chē

1.i	3rd vs. 2nd	chǔ	chú
		kě	ké
		xǐ	xí
		qǔ	qú

1.j	3rd vs. 4th	bǒ	bò
		nǐ	nì
		chǔ	chù
		rě	rè

1.k	4th vs. 1st	jì	jī
		là	lā
		sù	sū
		hè	hē

1.l	4th vs. 2nd	nà	ná
		zè	zé
		jù	jú
		lǜ	lǘ

1.m	4th vs. 3rd	sà	sǎ
		zì	zǐ
		kù	kǔ
		zhè	zhě

D.1 Practice II: Bisyllablic words

2.a	1st 1st:	chūzū	tūchū	chūfā
2.b	1st 2nd:	chátú	xīqí	chūxí
2.c	1st 3rd:	shēchǐ	gēqǔ	chūbǎn
2.d	1st 4th:	chūsè	hūshì	jīlù
2.e	2nd 1st:	shíshī	qíjī	shíchā
2.f	2nd 2nd:	jíhé	shépí	pígé
2.g	2nd 3rd:	jítǐ	bóqǔ	zhélǐ
2.h	2nd 4th:	qítè	fúlì	chíxù
2.i	3rd 1st:	zǔzhī	zhǔjī	lǐkē
2.j	3rd 2nd:	pǔjí	zhǔxí	chǔfá
2.k	3rd 4th:	lǚkè	gǔlì	tǐzhì
2.l	4th 1st:	zìsī	qìchē	lǜshī
2.m	4th 2nd:	fùzá	dìtú	shìshí
2.n	4th 3rd:	zìjǐ	bìhǔ	dìzhǐ
2.o	4th 4th:	mùdì	xùmù	dàdì

D.1 Practice III: Words with "er" sound

3.a	érzi	érqiě
3.b	ěrduo	mù'ěr
3.c	shí'èr	èrshí

D.2: Tone sandhi:

    If two third tone syllables are spoken in succession, the first third tone becomes second tone. This tone change is known as tone sandhi in linguistics. For instance,

xǐlǐ	-->	xílǐ	(baptism)
chǐrǔ	-->	chírǔ	(shame)
qǔshě	-->	qúshě	(accept or reject)

Note: In this book, when two third tone syllables are placed together, the tone marks will not be changed from third tone to second tone. However, the user should be aware that because of the tone sandhi, the first syllable actually is pronounced as a second tone syllable.

D.2 Practice:

chǔlǐ	--->	chúlǐ	gǔpǔ	--->	gúpǔ
bǐnǐ	--->	bínǐ	jǔzhǐ	--->	júzhǐ
zǐnǔ	--->	zínǔ	zhǐshǐ	--->	zhíshǐ

D.3: Neutral tone:

The neutral tone occurs in unstressed syllables. It is unmarked. For instance,

chēzi (car) **māma** (mom) **chúzi** (cook)

shūshu (uncle) **lǐzi** (plum) **shìzi** (persimmon)

The pitch of the neutral tone is determined by the preceding syllable.

D.3 Practice:

1. māma	gēge	shīfu	chūqu
2. dízi	bóbo	bízi	chúle
3. lǐzi	qǐzi	dǐzi	fǔshang
4. bàba	dìdi	kèqi	kùzi

E. Combination Exercises:

I.			
shān	xiān	sān	
cháng	qiáng	cáng	
zhǐ	jǐ	zǐ	
lüè	nüè	yuè	
kè	lè	rè	

II.			
Zhōngguó	xīngqī	lǜshī	zhàopiàn
zàijiàn	tóngxué	xǐhuan	diànshì
yīnyuè	kělè	yǎnlèi	shàngwǔ
cèsuǒ	chūntiān	xiàwǔ	bànyè
gōngkè	kāishǐ	rìjì	cāntīng
zuìjìn	xīwàng	yīsheng	chūzū
zhōumò	guānxi	dòufu	jiéhūn
liúxué	nǚ'ér	shénme	suīrán
wǎngqiú	xǐzǎo	niánjí	yóuyǒng

II. CHINESE WRITING SYSTEM

A. The Formation of Chinese Characters

Unlike English, which is an alphabetic language, Chinese writing is represented by "characters," and there are more than fifty thousand Chinese characters in existence. When tracing the history of character formation, they can be divided into the following six categories:

1. 象形　　xiàngxíng　　pictographs, pictographic characters

    Examples:

    人　(𝑅)　　rén　　man

    山　(⋒⋒)　　shān　　mountain

    日　(⊙)　　rì　　sun

    月　(☽)　　yuè　　moon

    木　(朩)　　mù　　tree

2. 指事　　zhǐshì　　self-explanatory

    Examples:

    上　(⌒)　　shàng　　above

    下　(⌣)　　xià　　below

3. 會意　　huìyì　　associative compounds

    Examples:

    明　(☽)　　míng　　bright

    休　(𝑅朩)　　xiū　　rest

4. 形聲　　xíngshēng　　pictophonetic characters (with one element indicating meaning and the other sound)

    Examples: 江，河，飯，姑

5. 轉注　　zhuǎnzhù　　mutually explanatory characters

    Examples: 老，考

6. 假借　　jiǎjiè　　phonetic loan characters

    Examples: 來，我

A popular myth is that Chinese writing is pictographic, and that each Chinese character represents a picture. It is true that some Chinese characters have evolved from pictures, but they only comprise a small part of the characters. The vast majority of Chinese characters are pictophonetic characters consisting of a radical and a phonetic element. The radical often suggests the meaning of a character, and the phonetic element indicates its original pronunciation which may, or may not, represent its modern pronunciation.

B. Basic Chinese Radicals

Although there are more than fifty thousand Chinese characters in existence, one only needs to know two or three thousand of them to be considered literate. Mastering two or three thousand characters is, of course, a rather formidable task. However, the learning process will be more effective and easier if one knows well the basic components of Chinese characters. Traditionally, Chinese characters are grouped together according to their common components known as "radicals" (部首, bùshǒu). There are 214 of them. By knowing the basic components and radicals well, you will find recognizing, remembering and reproducing characters much easier. Knowing the radicals is also a must when using dictionaries which arrange characters according to their radicals. The following is a selection of forty radicals which everybody should know well when starting to learn characters.

Chinese radical	*Pinyin*	*English*	*Examples*
1. 人 (亻)	rén	man	你，他
2. 刀 (刂)	dāo	knife	分，到
3. 力	lì	power	加，助
4. 又	yòu	right hand; again	友，取
5. 口	kǒu	mouth	叫，可
6. 囗**	wéi	enclose	回，因
7. 土	tǔ	earth	在，坐
8. 夕	xī	sunset	外，多
9. 大	dà	big	天，太
10. 女	nǚ	woman	好，媽
11. 子	zǐ	son	字，學
12. 寸	cùn	inch	對，專
13. 小	xiǎo	small	少，尖
14. 工	gōng	labor; work	左，差
15. 幺	yāo	tiny; small	幾，幼
16. 弓	gōng	bow	張，弟
17. 心 (忄)	xīn	heart	忙，快
18. 戈	gē	dagger-axe	我，或
19. 手 (扌)	shǒu	hand	打，找

20.	日	rì	sun	早，明
21.	月	yuè	moon	有，明
22.	木	mù	wood	李，杯
23.	水（氵）	shuǐ	water	沒，洗
24.	火（灬）	huǒ	fire	燒，熱
25.	田	tián	field	男，留
26.	目	mù	eye	看，睡
27.	示（礻）	shì	show	社，票
28.	糸（糹）**	mì	fine silk	紅，素
29.	耳	ěr	ear	聽，聊
30.	衣（衤）	yī	clothing	衫，裏
31.	言	yán	speech	說，認
32.	貝	bèi	cowry shell	貴，買
33.	走	zǒu	walk	趣，起
34.	足	zú	foot	跳，跑
35.	金	jīn	gold	錢，銀
36.	門	mén	door	問，間
37.	隹	zhuī	short-tailed bird	雖，難
38.	雨	yǔ	rain	電，雲
39.	食（飠）	shí	eat	飯，館
40.	馬	mǎ	horse	騎，驚

(** = used as radical only, not as a character by itself)

C. Basic Strokes

The following is a list of basic strokes:

Basic stroke	Chinese	Pinyin	English	Examples
1. " 丶 "	點	diǎn	dot	小，六
2. " 一 "	橫	héng	horizontal	一，六
3. " 丨 "	豎	shù	vertical	十，中
4. " 丿 "	撇	piě	downward left	人，大
5. " 乀 "	捺	nà	downward right	八，人
6. " ㇀ "	提	tí	upward	我，江
7. " 乛 "	橫鉤	hénggōu	horizontal hook	你，字

8. " 亅 "　　竪鈎　　　shùgōu　　　vertical hook　　　小 ，你

9. " ㇂ "　　斜鈎　　　xiégōu　　　slanted hook　　　戈 ，我

10. " ㇕ "　　橫折　　　héngzhé　　　horizontal bend　　　五 ，口

11. " ㄴ "　　竪折　　　shùzhé　　　vertical bend　　　七 ，亡

Note: With the exception of the "tí" stroke, which moves upward, all Chinese strokes move from top to bottom, and from left to right.

D. Stroke Order

     Following is a list of rules of stroke order. When writing a Chinese character, it is important that you follow the rules. Following the rules will make it easier for you to accurately count the number of strokes in a character. Knowing the exact number of strokes in a character will help you find the character in a radical-based dictionary. Also, your Chinese characters will look better if you write them in the correct stroke order!

1. From left to right　　　　　　（ 川 ，人 ）

2. From top to bottom　　　　　　（ 三 ）

3. Horizontal before vertical　　　（ 十 ）

4. From outside to inside　　　　　（ 月 ）

5. Middle before two sides　　　　（ 小 ）

6. Inside before closing　　　　　（ 日 ，回 ）

Note: Please learn the correct stroke orders of the characters introduced in this book by using the *Integrated Chinese Level One: Character Workbook.*

III. USEFUL EXPRESSIONS

A. Classroom Expressions

The following is a list of classroom expressions which you will hear everyday in your Chinese class.

1.	Nǐ hǎo!	How are you? How do you do?
2.	Lǎoshī hǎo!	How are you, teacher?
3.	Shàng kè.	Let's begin the class.
4.	Xià kè.	The class is over.
5.	Dǎ kāi shū.	Open the book.
6.	Wǒ shuō, nǐmen tīng.	I'll speak, you listen.
7.	Kàn hēibǎn.	Look at the blackboard.
8.	Duì bu duì?	Is it right?
9.	Duì!	Right! Correct!
10.	Hěn hǎo!	Very good!
11.	Qǐng gēn wǒ shuō.	Please repeat after me.
12.	Zài shuō yí cì.	Say it again.
13.	Dǒng bu dǒng?	Do you understand?
14.	Dǒng le.	Yes, I/we understand; I/we do.
15.	Zàijiàn!	Good-bye!

B. Survival Expressions

The following is a list of important expressions which will help you survive in a Chinese language environment. A good language student is constantly learning new words by asking questions. Learn the following expressions well and start to acquire Chinese on your own!

1.	Duìbuqǐ!	Sorry!
2.	Qǐng wèn ...	Excuse me ...; May I ask ...
3.	Xièxie!	Thanks!
4.	Zhè shi shénme?	What is this?
5.	Wǒ bù dǒng.	I don't understand.
6.	Qǐng zài shuō yí biàn.	Please say it one more time.
7.	"..." Zhōngguóhuà zěnme shuō?	How do you say "..." in Chinese?
8.	"..." shì shénme yìsi?	What does "..." mean?
9.	Qǐng nǐ gěi wǒ ...	Please give me ...
10.	Qǐng nǐ gàosu wǒ ...	Please tell me ...

C. Numerals

Having a good control of the Chinese numerials will facilitate your dealing with real life situations such as shopping, asking for time and dates, etc. You can get a head start by memorizing 1 to 10 well now.

1.	yī	one	一
2.	èr	two	二
3.	sān	three	三
4.	sì	four	四
5.	wǔ	five	五
6.	liù	six	六
7.	qī	seven	七
8.	bā	eight	八
9.	jiǔ	nine	九
10.	shí	ten	十

Do you know the names of the strokes below? Can you write them properly?

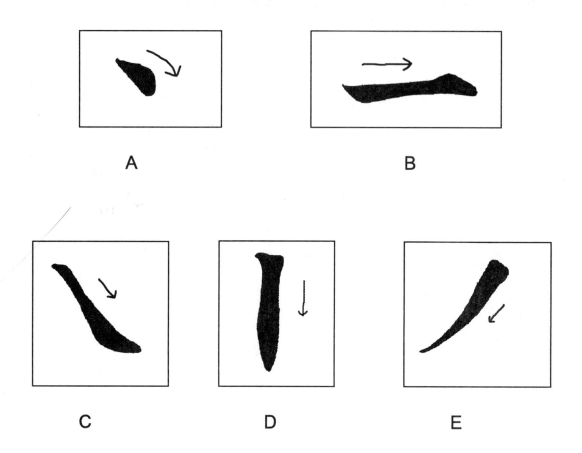

A

B

C

D

E

關你老母

幹你媽
gan ni ma

Lesson One   Greetings
第一課   問好

DIALOGUE I: *EXCHANGING GREETINGS*

Vocabulary

先   問   老師

1. 先生 xiānsheng   N   Mr.

2. 你好 nǐ hǎo   CE   How do you do? Hello!

   你 nǐ   Pr   you

   好 hǎo   Adj   fine; good; nice; O.K.

3. 小姐 xiǎojie   N   Miss; young lady

4. 請問 qǐng wèn   CE   May I ask...

   請 qǐng   V   please (polite form of request)

21

	問	wèn	V	to ask
5.	您	nín	Pr	you (polite)
6.	貴姓	guì xìng	CE	What is your honorable surname?
	貴	guì	Adj	honorable
	姓	xìng	V/N	(one's) surname is.../ surname
7.	我	wǒ	Pr	I; me
8.	呢	ne	QP	(a particle)
9.	叫	jiào	V	to be called
10.	什麼	shénme	QPr	what
11.	名字	míngzi	N	name

Proper Nouns

12.	王朋	Wáng Péng		(a person's name)
	王	wáng	N	(a surname); king
13.	李友	Lǐ Yǒu		(a person's name)
	李	lǐ	N	(a surname); plum

Dialogue I: *Pinyin*

Wáng xiānsheng [1] :   Nǐ hǎo [2]!

Lǐ xiǎojie: Nǐ hǎo !

Wáng xiānsheng: Qǐng wèn, nín guì xìng [3]?

Lǐ xiǎojie: Wǒ xìng [G1] Lǐ. Nǐ ne [G2]?

Wáng xiānsheng: Wǒ xìng Wáng, jiào [G3] Wáng Péng. Nǐ jiào shénme

                     míngzi [4]?

Lǐ xiǎojie: Wǒ jiào Lǐ Yǒu.

Dialogue I: *Chinese*

王先生[1] ： 你好[2] ！

李小姐 ： 你好！

王先生 ： 請問，您貴姓[3] ？

李小姐 ： 我<u>姓</u>[G1]李。你<u>呢</u>[G2] ？

王先生 ： 我姓王，<u>叫</u>[G3] 王朋。你叫什麼名字[4] ？

李小姐 ： 我叫李友。

Notes:

(1) In Chinese one's surname precedes one's given name. The number of Chinese family names is fairly limited. The most common ones number around a hundred. Personal names almost always carry positive meaning. When addressing an unfamiliar person, it is best to call him or her 先生 (xiānsheng, Mr.) or 小姐 (xiǎojie, Miss). It is rather impolite to use the full name. In most areas in China, given names are used only by one's close friends, parents, spouse, and elder siblings.

(2) The expression "你好！" (Nǐ hǎo!) is a popular form of greeting. It can be used when two persons meet for the first time in the same manner as English speakers say "How do you do!" or used by people who have met before to exchange greetings. "你好！" (Nǐ hǎo!) is usually answered with "你好！" (Nǐ hǎo!) The expression "你好嗎？" (Nǐ hǎo ma? How are you?) is a greeting in the form of a question, and it is usually answered with "我很好." (Wǒ hěn hǎo. I am fine.) Due to tone *sandhi*, the 你 (nǐ) in "你好！" (Nǐ hǎo!) is pronounced with second tone (ní) rather than the original third tone (nǐ). For the same reason 小 (xiǎo) in 小姐 (xiǎojie, Miss) is also pronounced as second tone rather the original third tone. As mentioned in the introduction, this textbook does NOT change a tone mark from third tone to second tone to reflect tone *sandhi*. Please always bear in mind that when a third tone syllable follows another, the first one will become second tone.

(3) In China, when you first meet a person, it is polite to ask for his/her last name, rather than his/her full name.

(4) When the last name is known, the phrase "你叫什麼名字？" (Nǐ jiào shénme míngzi? What is your name?) is used to find out a person's given name. Otherwise, it is used to find out the full name of the person.

Do you know anybody with the following surnames?

畢 (Bì); 蔡 (Cài); 陳 (Chén); 高 (Gāo); 黃 (Huáng); 李 (Lǐ); 林 (Lín); 劉 (Liú); 羅 (Ló); 毛 (Máo); 史 (Shǐ); 王 (Wáng); 吳 (Wú); 謝 (Xiè); 徐 (Xú), 許 (Xǔ); 楊 (Yáng); 姚 (Yáo); 葉 (Yè); 張 (Zhāng); 鄭 (Zhèng); 周 (Zhōu)

DIALOGUE II: *ASKING ONE'S STATUS*

Vocabulary

1.	是	shì	V	to be
2.	老師	lǎoshī	N	teacher
3.	嗎	ma	QP	(a particle)
4.	不	bù	Adv	not; no
5.	學生	xuésheng	N	student
6.	也	yě	Adv	too; also
7.	中國人	Zhōngguórén	N	Chinese people/person
	中國	Zhōngguó	N	China
	人	rén	N	people; person
8.	美國人	Měiguórén	N	American people/person
	美國	Měiguó	N	the United States of America

Dialogue II: *Pinyin*

Lǐ xiǎojie: Wáng xiānsheng, nǐ <u>shì</u> [G4] lǎoshī <u>ma</u> [G5]?

Wáng xiānsheng: <u>Bù</u> [G6], wǒ bú [1] shì lǎoshī, wǒ shì xuésheng. Lǐ xiǎojie, nǐ ne?

Lǐ xiǎojie: Wǒ <u>yě</u> [G7] shì xuésheng. Nǐ shì Zhōngguórén ma?

Wáng xiānsheng: Shì, wǒ shì Zhōngguórén. Nǐ shì Měiguórén ma?

Lǐ xiǎojie: Wǒ shì Měiguórén.

Dialogue II: *Chinese*

李小姐：王先生，你是^(G4)老師嗎^(G5)？

王先生：不^(G6)，我不⁽¹⁾是老師，我是學生。李
小姐，你呢？

李小姐：我也^(G7)是學生。你是中國人嗎？

王先生：是，我是中國人。你是美國人嗎？

李小姐：我是美國人。

Notes:

(1) The basic pronunciation for 不 is "bù" with fourth tone. However, when it is placed before another fourth tone syllable, 不 is pronounced in the second tone instead. Therefore, 不是 is pronounced "bú shì" rather than "bù shì." In this textbook, the tone for 不 is marked as it is actually pronounced.

Supplementary Vocabulary

1. 朋友	péngyou	N	friend
2. 太太	tàitai	N	wife; Mrs.
3. 英國	Yīngguó	N	Britain; England
4. 法國	Fǎguó	N	France
5. 日本	Rìběn	N	Japan
6. 德國	Déguó	N	Germany
7. 英國人	Yīngguórén	N	British people/person
8. 法國人	Fǎguórén	N	French people/person
9. 日本人	Rìběnrén	N	Japanese people/person
10. 德國人	Déguórén	N	German people/person

GRAMMAR

1. The Verb 姓 (xìng)

姓 (xìng) is both a noun and a verb. When it is used as a verb, it must be followed by an object.
For example:

(1) 你姓什麼？

Nǐ xìng shénme?

(What is your surname?)

(2) 我姓王。

Wǒ xìng Wáng.

(My surname is Wang.)

姓 (xìng) is usually negated with 不 (bù).

(3) 我不姓李。

Wǒ bú xìng Lǐ.

(My surname is not Li.)

2. Questions Ending with 呢 (ne)

呢 (ne) often follows a noun or pronoun to form a question when the content of the question is already clear from the context.
For example:

(1) 我是中國人，你呢？

Wǒ shì Zhōngguórén, nǐ ne?

(I am Chinese. How about you?)

(2) 他是老師，你呢？

Tā shì lǎoshī, nǐ ne?

(He is a teacher. How about you?)

Note: When 呢 (ne) is used in this way, there must be some context. In sentence (1) the context is provided by the preceding sentence, "我是中國人." (Wǒ shì Zhōngguórén.) In sentence (2), as well, "他是老師." (Tā shì lǎoshī.) provides the context.

3. The Verb 叫 (jiào)

The verb 叫 (jiào) has several meanings. It means "to be called" in this lesson. It must be followed by an object.
For example:

(1) 你叫什麼名字？

Nǐ jiào shénme míngzi?

(What is your name?)

(2) 我叫李生。

Wǒ jiào Lǐ Shēng.

(My name is Li Sheng.)

叫 (jiào) is usually negated with 不 (bù).

(3) 我不叫李生。

Wǒ bú jiào Lǐ Shēng.

(My name is not Li Sheng.)

4. The Verb 是 (shì)

In Chinese, 是 (shì) is a verb which can be used to link two nouns, pronouns, or noun phrases that are in some way equivalent.
For example:

(1) 李友是學生。

Lǐ Yǒu shì xuésheng.

(Li You is a student.)

(2) 我是老師。

Wǒ shì lǎoshī.

(I am a teacher.)

(3) 你是美國人嗎？

Nǐ shì Měiguórén ma?

(Are you an American?)

是 (shì) is usually negated with 不 (bù).

(4) 李友不是中國人。

      Lǐ Yǒu bú shì Zhōngguórén.

      (Li You is not Chinese.)

(5) 王朋不是老師。

      Wáng Péng bú shì lǎoshī.

      (Wang Peng is not a teacher.)

5. Questions Ending with 嗎 (ma)

When 嗎 (ma) is added to the end of a descriptive statement, that statement is turned into a question. The person who asks a question that ends with 嗎 (ma) often has some expectation of the answer. In sentence (1) below, the questioner may expect that the other person is a teacher, and in sentence (2) the questioner may expect that the other person is a student. To answer the question in the affirmative, 是 (shì) is used while 不 (bù) is used in a negative answer.

For example:

(1) 你是老師嗎 ？

      Nǐ shì lǎoshī ma?

      (Are you a teacher?)

   A: 是，我是老師。

      Shì, wǒ shì lǎoshī.

      (Yes, I am a teacher.)

   B: 不，我不是老師。

      Bù, wǒ bú shì lǎoshī.

      (No, I am not a teacher.)

   C: 不，我是學生。

      Bù, wǒ shì xuésheng.

      (No, I am a student.)

(2) 王友是學生嗎？

Wáng Yǒu shì xuésheng ma?

(Is Wang You a student?)

A: 是，王友是學生。

Shì, Wáng Yǒu shì xuésheng.

(Yes, Wang You is a student.)

B: 不，王友不是學生。

Bù, Wáng Yóu bú shì xuésheng.

(No, Wang You is not a student.)

C: 不，王友是老師。

Bù, Wáng Yǒu shì lǎoshī.

(No, Wang You is a teacher.)

(3) 李朋是美國人嗎？

Lǐ Péng shì Měiguórén ma?

(Is Li Peng an American?)

A: 是，李朋是美國人。

Shì, Lǐ Péng shì Měiguórén.

(Yes, Li Peng is an American.)

B: 不，李朋不是美國人。

Bù, Lǐ Péng bú shì Měiguórén.

(No, Li Peng is not an American.)

C: 不，李朋是中國人。

Bù, Lí Péng shì Zhōngguórén.

(No, Li Peng is Chinese.)

6. The Negative Adverb 不 (bù)

In Chinese there are two main negative adverbs. 不 (bù), one of the two, is used in this lesson.

For example:

(1) 李友不是中國人。

    Lǐ Yǒu bú shì Zhōngguórén.

    (Li You is not Chinese.)

(2) 我不姓王。

    Wǒ bú xìng Wáng.

    (My surname is not Wang.)

(3) 我不叫李中。

    Wǒ bú jiào Lǐ Zhōng.

    (My name is not Li Zhong.)

7. The Adverb 也 (yě)

The adverb 也 (yě) basically means "too, also" in English. In Chinese adverbs normally appear after subjects and in front of verbs. They usually cannot precede subjects or follow verbs. The adverb 也 (yě) cannot be put before the subject or at the very end of a sentence.

For example:

(1) 王朋是學生，李友也是學生。

    Wáng Péng shì xuésheng, Lǐ Yǒu yě shì xuésheng.

    (Wang Peng is a student. Li You is a student, too.)

(2) 你是中國人，我也是中國人。

    Nǐ shì Zhōngguórén, wǒ yě shì Zhōngguórén.

    (You are Chinese, and I am also Chinese.)

The following sentences are incorrect:

(2a) **Incorrect:** 你是中國人，我是中國人也。

    Nǐ shì Zhōngguórén, wǒ shì Zhōngguórén yě.

(2b) **Incorrect:** 你是中國人，也我是中國人。

    Nǐ shì Zhōngguórén, yě wǒ shì Zhōngguórén.

PATTERN DRILLS

[**Note:** All the exercises in the Pattern Drills section of each lesson are meant to be **Substitution Drills** unless otherwise noted. The teacher first says a sentence, then gives one or two word(s). The student should use the word(s) to form a new sentence.]

A. 是 (shì)

| Example: | Teacher: Wǒ <u>shì</u> lǎoshī. (xuésheng) |
| | Student: Wǒ <u>shì</u> xuésheng. |

Teacher: 我<u>是</u>老師。 （學生）

Student: 我<u>是</u>學生。

1.	Wǒ	<u>shì</u>	Zhōngguó xuésheng.
2.	Nǐ		lǎoshī.
3.	Lǐ xiǎojie		xuésheng.
4.	Wáng xiānsheng		lǎoshī.
5.	Wáng Péng		Zhōngguórén.
6.	Lǐ Yǒu		Měiguórén.

1.	我	<u>是</u>	中國學生。
2.	你		老師。
3.	李小姐		學生。
4.	王先生		老師。
5.	王朋		中國人。
6.	李友		美國人。

B. 是...嗎 (shì...ma)

1. Wáng xiānsheng	<u>shì</u>	xuésheng	ma?
2. Lǐ Yǒu		Zhōngguórén	
3. Wáng Péng		Měiguórén	
4. Lǐ xiǎojie		Zhōngguó xuésheng	
5. Wáng xiānsheng		Měiguó lǎoshī	

1. 王先生   <u>是</u>   學生   嗎 ？

2. 李友   中國人

3. 王朋   美國人

4. 李小姐   中國學生

5. 王先生   美國老師

C. 嗎 (ma)

(Provide appropriate questions in column A for the answers in column B.)

Example: A: <u>Nǐ shì Wáng Péng ma?</u>   B: Bù, wǒ bú shì Wáng Péng.

    A：<u>你是王朋嗎？</u>   B：不，我不是王朋。

1. A: _____ ?   B: Bù, Wáng Péng bú shì lǎoshī.
2. A: _____ ?   B: Lǐ Yǒu shì xuésheng.
3. A: _____ ?   B: Wáng Péng shì Zhōngguórén.
4. A: _____ ?   B: Bù, Lǐ Yǒu bú shì Zhōngguórén.
5. A: _____ ?   B: Bù, wǒ bú xìng Lǐ.
6. A: _____ ?   B: Bù, wǒ bú jiào Lǐ Yǒu, wǒ jiào Wáng
                                                       Yǒu.

1. A：_____ ?   B：不，王朋不是老師。

2. A：_____ ?   B：李友是學生。

3. A：_____ ?   B：王朋是中國人。

4. A：_____ ?   B：不，李友不是中國人。

5. A：_____ ?   B：不，我不姓李。

6. A：_____ ?   B：不，我不叫李友，我叫
                                                       王友。

D. 也 (yě)

1. <u>Nǐ shì</u>	xuésheng,	wǒ	<u>yě shì</u>	xuésheng.
2.	lǎoshī,	Wáng xiānsheng		lǎoshī.
3.	Zhōngguórén,	Lǐ xiǎojie		Zhōngguórén.
4.	Měiguórén,	Wáng xiǎojie		Měiguórén.
5.	xuésheng,	Wáng xiānshēng		xuésheng.
6.	lǎoshī,	Lǐ xiānsheng		lǎoshī.

1. <u>你是</u>	學生，	我	<u>也是</u>	學生。
2.	老師，	王先生		老師。
3.	中國人，	李小姐		中國人。
4.	美國人，	王小姐		美國人。
5.	學生，	王先生		學生。
6.	老師，	李先生		老師。

E. 不 (bù) (Answer questions with 不 .)

Example:　Nǐ shì lǎoshī ma?　　-->　　Wǒ <u>bú</u> shì lǎoshī.

你是老師嗎？ --> 我<u>不</u>是老師。

1. Lǐ Yǒu shì Zhōngguórén ma?
2. Nǐ shì Wáng lǎoshī ma?
3. Wáng Péng shì Měiguórén ma?
4. Nǐ jiào Lǐ yǒu ma?
5. Lǎoshī xìng Wáng ma?

1. 李友是中國人嗎？

2. 你是王老師嗎？

3. 王朋是美國人嗎？

4. 你叫李友嗎？

5. 老師姓王嗎？

F. 是···不是··· (shì ... bú shì ...)

1. <u>Wǒ shì</u>	Lǐ Yǒu,	<u>bú shì</u>	Wáng Péng.
2.	Zhōngguórén,		Měiguórén.
3.	xuésheng,		lǎoshī.
4.	Zhōngguó xuésheng,		Měiguó xuésheng.
5.	Wáng xiānsheng,		Lǐ xiānsheng.
6.	Lǐ xiǎojie,		Wáng xiǎojie.
7.	Lǐ lǎoshī		Wáng lǎoshī.

1. <u>我是</u>　　　李友，　　<u>不是</u>　　　王朋。

2. 　　　　　　中國人，　　　　　　　美國人。

3. 　　　　　　學生，　　　　　　　　老師。

4. 　　　　　　中國學生，　　　　　　美國學生。

5. 　　　　　　王先生，　　　　　　　李先生。

6. 　　　　　　李小姐，　　　　　　　王小姐。

7. 　　　　　　李老師，　　　　　　　王老師。

G. 呢 (ne)

1. <u>Wǒ shì</u>	Zhōngguórén,	nǐ	<u>ne</u>?
2.	Měiguórén,	Wáng xiǎojie	
3.	xuésheng,	Lǐ xiānsheng	
4.	Měiguórén,	Wáng lǎoshī	
5.	lǎoshī,	Lǐ xiǎojie	

1. <u>我是</u>　　　中國人，　　　你　　　<u>呢</u>？

2. 　　　　　　美國人，　　　王小姐

3. 　　　　　　學生，　　　　李先生

4. 　　　　　　美國人，　　　王老師

5. 　　　　　　老師，　　　　李小姐

PRONUNCIATION EXERCISES

A. Practice the following initials:

1.	b	p	d	t
	bǎo	pǎo	dā	tā
	bān	pān	dí	tí
	bù	pù	duì	tuì
	bō	pō	dīng	tīng
	bēng	pēng	děng	téng

2.	j	q	z	c
	jiǎo	qiǎo	zāi	cāi
	jǐng	qǐng	zǎo	cǎo
	jīn	qīn	zì	cì
	jiě	qiě	zé	cè
	jiàn	qiàn	zhè	chè

3.	sh	s	x
	shēn	sēn	xīn
	shēng	sēng	xīng
	shàn	sàn	xiàn
	shà	sàng	xià

B. Practice the following tones:

tiāntiān	jīnnián	jīnglǐ	shēngqì
xīngqī	fādá	fāzhǎn	shēngdiào

C. Practice the following syllables with neutral tones:

xiānsheng	míngzi	xiǎojie	shénme
wǒ de	nǐ de	tā de	shéi de

D. Practice the following tones:

nǐ hǎo	Lǐ Yǒu	lǎohǔ	zhǎnlǎn
hǎo duō	nǐ lái	hǎo shū	qǐng wèn

ENGLISH TEXT

Dialogue I

Mr. Wang:	How do you do?
Miss Li:	How do you do?
Mr. Wang:	What is your family name, please?
Miss Li:	My family name is Li. What is yours?
Mr. Wang:	My family name is Wang. My name is Wang Peng. What is your name?
Miss Li:	My name is Li You.

Dialogue II

Miss Li:	Mr. Wang, are you a teacher?
Mr. Wang:	No, I'm not a teacher. I am a student. How about you, Miss Li?
Miss Li.	I am a student, too. Are you Chinese?
Mr. Wang:	Yes, I am Chinese. Are you American?
Miss Li:	I'm American.

Can you tell their nationalities by their costumes?

Lesson Two   Family
第二課   家庭

DIALOGUE I: *LOOKING AT A FAMILY PHOTO*

Vocabulary

1. 那	nà/nèi	Pr	that
2. 張	zhāng	M	(a measure word for flat objects)
3. 照片	zhàopiàn	N	picture; photo
4. 的	de		(indicating a possessive or a qualifying or descriptive word or phrase)
5. 這	zhè/zhèi	Pr	this

6.	爸爸	bàba	N	dad
7.	媽媽	māma	N	mom
8.	個	gè	M	(the measure word which is most extensively used)
9.	男孩子	nánháizi	N	boy
	男	nán	N	male
	孩子	háizi	N	child
10.	誰	shéi	QPr	who
11.	他	tā	Pr	he; him (It may mean either "he/him" or "she/her" when the sex of the person is unknown.)
12.	弟弟	dìdi	N	younger brother
13.	女孩子	nǚháizi	N	girl
	女	nǚ	N	female
14.	妹妹	mèimei	N	younger sister
15.	她	tā	Pr	she
16.	女兒	nǚ'ér	N	daughter
17.	有	yǒu	V	to have; there is/are
18.	兒子	érzi	N	son
19.	沒	méi	Adv	not

Proper Nouns

20.	小高	Xiǎo Gāo		Little Gao
	小	xiǎo		small; little
	高	gāo		(a surname); tall

Dialogue I: *Pinyin*

(Wang Peng is in Little Gao's room pointing to a picture on the wall.)

Wáng Péng: Xiǎo Gāo [1], nà zhāng [G1] zhàopiàn shì nǐ de ma?

(They both walk toward the picture and then stand in front of it.)

Xiǎo Gāo: Shì. Zhè shì wǒ bàba, zhè shì wǒ māma.

Wáng Péng: Zhège nánháizi shì shéi [G2]?

Xiǎo Gāo: Tā shì wǒ dìdi.

Wáng Péng: Zhège nǚháizi shì nǐ mèimei ma?

Xiǎo Gāo: Bú shì, tā shì Lǐ xiānsheng de nǚ'er.

Wáng Péng: Lǐ xiānsheng yǒu [G3] érzi ma?

Xiǎo Gāo: Tā méiyǒu érzi.

Dialogue I: *Chinese*

(Wang Peng is in Little Gao's room pointing to a picture on the wall.)

王朋：小高 [1]，那張 [G1] 照片是你的嗎？

(They both walk toward the picture and then stand in front of it.)

小高：是。這是我爸爸，這是我媽媽。

王朋：這個男孩子是誰 [G2]？

小高：他是我弟弟。　　　言隹

王朋：這個女孩子是你妹妹嗎？

小高：不是，她是李先生的女兒。

王朋：李先生有 [G3] 兒子嗎？

小高：他沒有兒子。

Notes:

(1) A familiar and affectionate way of addressing young people is to add the word 小 (xiǎo, little; small) to the surname, e.g., 小王 (Xiǎo Wǎng, Little Wang), 小李 (Xiǎo Lǐ, Little Li), 小高 (Xiǎo Gāo, Little Gao), etc. Similarly, to address a person above the middle age, the word 老 (lǎo, old) can be used to precede the surname, e.g., 老王 (Lǎo Wǎng, Old Wang), 老李 (Lǎo Lǐ, Old Li), 老高 (Lǎo Gāo, Old Gao), etc. However, such appellations are usually not used in addressing a relative or someone senior in social position.

DIALOGUE II: *ASKING ABOUT ONE'S FAMILY*

Vocabulary

1.	家	jiā	N	family; home
2.	幾	jǐ	QW	how many
3.	哥哥	gēge	N	older brother
4.	兩	liǎng	Nu	two; a couple of
4.	姐姐	jiějie	N	older sister
5.	和	hé	Conj	and
6.	做	zuò	V	to do
7.	英文	Yīngwén	N	English (language)
8.	律師	lǜshī	N	lawyer
9.	都	dōu	Adv	both; all
10.	大學生	dàxuéshēng	N	college student
	大學	dàxué	N	university; college
11.	醫生	yīshēng	N	doctor; physician

Proper Nouns

12.	小張	Xiǎo Zhāng		Little Zhang
	張	zhāng		(a surname)

On the Chinese School System

In China and Taiwan, the school system is somewhat similar to that in the United States. A typical education consists of six years of elementary school (小學, xiǎoxué, Grades 1-6), six years of middle school (中學, zhōngxué, Grades 7-12), and four years of university or college (學院, xuéyuàn). Middle school is further divided into junior high (初中, chūzhōng, Grades 7-9) and senior high (高中, gāozhōng, Grades 10-12). Many students also attend kindergarten before they enter the grade school, and some of them continue into graduate school after college. Now that you have learned that a college student is called 大學生 (dàxuéshēng) in Chinese, can you guess the words for elementary school students, junior high school students, and senior high students?

Dialogue II: *Pinyin*

Lǐ Yǒu: Xiǎo Zhāng, nǐ jiā yǒu (G4) jǐ (1) ge rén?

Xiǎo Zhāng: Wǒ jiā yǒu liù ge rén. Wǒ bàba, wǒ māma (2), yí (3) ge (4) gēge, liǎng (G5) ge jiějie hé wǒ. Lǐ xiǎojie, nǐ jiā yǒu jǐ ge rén?

Lǐ Yǒu: Wǒ jiā yǒu wǔ ge rén: bàba, māma, liǎng ge mèimei hé wǒ. Nǐ bàba māma shì zuò shénme de (5)?

Xiǎo Zhāng: Wǒ māma shì Yīngwén lǎoshī, bàba shì lǜshī, gēge jiějie dōu (G6) shì dàxuéshēng.

Lǐ Yǒu: Wǒ māma yě shì lǎoshī, wǒ bàba shì yīshēng.

(Is this the Zhang family or the Li family?)

Dialogue II: *Chinese*

李友：小張，你家有^(G4)幾個⁽¹⁾人？

小張：我家有六個人。我爸爸、我媽媽⁽²⁾、一⁽³⁾
　　　個⁽⁴⁾哥哥、兩^(G5)個姐姐和我。李小姐，你
　　　家有幾個人？

李友：我家有五個人。爸爸、媽媽、兩個妹妹和
　　　我。你爸爸媽媽是做什麼的⁽⁵⁾？

小張：我媽媽是英文老師，爸爸是律師，哥哥、
　　　姐姐都^(G6)是大學生。

李友：我媽媽也是老師，我爸爸是醫生。

Notes:

(1) For the number of people in a family, another measure word 口 (kǒu) is also used.

(2) In Chinese, it is customary to mention the male before the female. Therefore, one says, 爸爸、媽媽，哥哥、姐姐，弟弟、妹妹 (bàba, māma, gēge, jiějie, dìdi, mèimei) instead of 媽媽、爸爸，姐姐、哥哥，妹妹、弟弟 (māma, bàba, jiějie, gēge, mèimei, dìdi), etc.

(3) The numeral "一" (one) is pronounced with first tone "yī" when it stands alone or comes at the end of a word or sentence. Otherwise, it's pronunciation changes according to the following rules. (a) "yī" before a fourth tone syllable becomes second tone. Therefore, "一個" is pronounced "yí gè" rather than "yī gè." (b) "yī" before a syllable in any tone other than the fourth tone becomes fourth tone. The above rules also apply to the numerials "七" (qī, seven) and "八" (bā, eight). However, nowadays most of the people do not change tones when pronouncing "七" (qī, seven) and "八" (bā, eight).

(4) The original tone for the measure word 個 (gè) is the falling tone. However, in actual speech it is always pronounced as a neutral tone word.

(5) The expression " X 是做什麼的" (X shì zuò shénme de) is often used to ask for a person's occupation. "是...的" (shì...de) as a structure will be treated more fully later.

GRAMMAR

1. Measure Words (I)

Unlike in English, in Chinese a numeral usually cannot be immediately followed by a noun. Rather, a measure word has to be used in between. There are over a hundred measure words in Chinese, but only less than twenty are commonly used. The association of a measure word with a noun is not random but fixed according to the general meaning of the noun. The following are two measure words that we have learned in this lesson.

個 (gè): " 個 "(gè) is the single most commonly used measure word in Chinese. It is sometimes used as a substitute for other measure words.
Examples:

(1)	一個人	yí ge rén	a person
(2)	一個學生	yí ge xuésheng	a student
(3)	一個老師	yí ge lǎoshī	a teacher

張 (zhāng): This measure word is associated with objects that are characterized by a flat surface.
Examples:

(1)	一張照片	yì zhāng zhàopiàn	a photo
(2)	一張紙 (zhǐ)	yì zhāng zhǐ	a piece of paper
(3)	一張床 (chuáng)	yì zhāng chuáng	a bed

2. Question Pronouns

Interrogative pronouns include 誰 (shéi, who), 什麼 (shénme, what), 哪 (nǎ/něi, which), 哪兒 (nǎr, where), 幾 (jǐ, how many, which), etc. In a question with an interrogative pronoun, the word order is exactly the same as that in a non-interrogative statement. Therefore, when learning to compose a question in Chinese, one can start with a statement and then replace part of the statement that one wishes to ask about with the appropriate interrogative pronoun.
For example:

(1) 她是李友。

Tā shì Lǐ Yǒu.

(She is Li You.)

One can replace 她 (tā) with 誰 (shéi):

(2) 誰是李友？

　　Shéi shì Lǐ Yǒu?

　　(Who is Li You?)

誰 (shéi) functions as the subject of the sentence and occupies the same position as 她 (tā) in the corresponding statement.　Or one can replace 李友 (Lǐ Yǒu):

(3) 她是誰？

　　Tā shì shéi?

　　(Who is she?)

誰 (shéi) functions as the object of the sentence and occupies the same position as 李友 (Lǐ Yǒu).

Other examples:

(4) A: 我媽媽是醫生。

　　　Wǒ māma shì yīshēng.

　　　(My mother is a doctor.)

　B: 你媽媽做什麼？

　　　Nǐ māma zuò shénme?

　　　(What does your mother do?)

Examples with the verb 有 (yǒu).

(5) A: 王朋有妹妹。

　　　Wáng Péng yǒu mèimei.

　　　(Wang Peng has a younger sister.)

　B: 誰有妹妹？

　　　Shéi yǒu mèimei?

　　　(Who has a younger sister?)

(6) A: 我有三個姐姐。

　　　Wǒ yǒu sān ge jiějie.

　　　(I have three older sisters.)

B: 你有幾個姐姐？

Nǐ yǒu jǐ ge jiějie?

(How many older sisters do you have?)

Note: From the examples above, we can see that the basic word order in a Chinese sentence runs like this:

Subject + Verb + Object

The word order remains the same in statements and in questions. Please remember that you don't place the question word at the beginning of the question as you do in English, unless that question word serves as the subject.

3. 有 (yǒu) in the sense of "To have" or "To possess"

有 (yǒu) is always negated with 沒 (méi).

Examples:

(1) A: 王先生有一個弟弟。

Wáng xiānsheng yǒu yí ge dìdi.

(Mr. Wang has a younger brother.)

B: 王先生沒有弟弟。

Wáng xiānsheng méiyǒu dìdi.

(Mr. Wang doesn't have any younger brothers.)

(2) A: 我有兩張照片。

Wǒ yǒu liǎng zhāng zhàopiàn.

(I have two photos.)

B: 我沒有照片。

Wǒ méiyǒu zhàopiàn.

(I don't have any photos.)

4. 有 (yǒu) in the sense of Existence

Example: 我家有五個人。

Wǒ jiā yǒu wǔ ge rén.

(There are five people in my family.)

5. The Usage of 二 (èr) and 兩 (liǎng)

The words 二 (èr) and 兩 (liǎng) both mean "two," but they differ in usage. 兩 (liǎng) is used in front of common measure words. That is when the quantity of something is stated, e.g., 兩個人 (liǎng ge rén, two persons); when counting numbers, use "二" (èr) such as in "一，二，三，四……" (yī, èr, sān, sì, one, two, three, four...). Also, use "二" (èr) when the number occurs in the middle or at the end of a numerical series; e.g., 二十二 (èrshí'èr, twenty-two) and 一百二十五 (yìbǎi èrshíwǔ, 125).

Cases involving quadruple digit numbers will be introduced later.

6. 都 (dōu, both; all)

The adverb 都 (dōu) suggests inclusiveness. It refers to the preceding words, and therefore must be used at the end of an enumeration.

Examples:

(1) 王朋、高生和李友都是律師。

Wáng Péng, Gāo Shēng hé Lǐ Yǒu dōu shì lǜshī.

(Wang Peng, Gao Sheng and Li You are all lawyers.)

[都 (dōu) refers back to Wang Peng, Gao Sheng and Li You and therefore appears <u>after</u> they are mentioned.]

(2) 王朋和李友都不是老師。

Wáng Péng hé Lǐ Yǒu dōu bú shì lǎoshī.

(Neither Wang Peng nor Li You is a teacher.)

(3) 王朋和李友都有弟弟。

Wáng Péng hé Lǐ Yǒu dōu yǒu dìdi.

(Both Wang Peng and Li You have younger brothers.)

(4) 高生和張中都沒有妹妹。

Gāo Shēng hé Zhāng Zhōng dōu méi yǒu mèimei.

(Neither Gao Sheng nor Zhang Zhong has younger sisters.)

Note: 沒 (méi) is always used to negate 有 (yǒu). However, to express "not all of ... have" "不都有" (bù dōu yǒu), rather than "沒都有" (méi dōu yǒu), should be used. Whether the negator precedes or follows the word 都 (dōu), makes the difference between partial negation and entire negation. Compare:

a. 他們不都是中國人。

   (Tāmen bù dōu shì Zhōngguórén.)   (Not all of them are Chinese.)

b. 他們都不是中國人。

   (Tāmen dōu bù shì Zhōngguórén.)   (None of them are Chinese.)

Do you know what they do?

Do you have any family members or friends who have the above three kinds of jobs?

Please answer the questions in Chinese.

PATTERN DRILLS

A. 有 (yǒu, to have) with measure words

1. Wǒ	yǒu	yí	ge	gēge.
2. Tā		liǎng		jiějie.
3. Xiǎo Wáng		sān		mèimei.
4. Xiǎo Lǐ		yí		dìdi.
5. Xiǎo Zhāng		liǎng		Zhōngguó lǎoshī.
6. Gāo lǎoshī		sān		érzi.
7. Wǒ		liù	zhāng	zhàopiàn.

1. 我	有	一	個	哥哥。
2. 他		兩		姐姐。
3. 小王		三		妹妹。
4. 小李		一		弟弟。
5. 小張		兩		中國老師。
6. 高老師		三		兒子。
7. 我		六	張	照片。

B. 沒有 (méiyǒu, have not)

1. Lǎo Wáng yǒu	gēge,	méiyǒu	dìdi.
2.	jiějie		mèimei.
3.	Zhōngguó péngyǒu,		Měiguó péngyǒu.
4.	gēge,		jiějie.
5.	dìdi,		mèimei.
6.	mèimei,		jiějie.
7.	jiějie,		dìdi.
8.	nǚ'er,		érzi.

1. 老王 有	哥哥，	沒有	弟弟。
2.	姐姐，		妹妹。
3.	中國朋友，		美國朋友。
4.	哥哥，		姐姐。

5. <u>老王 有</u>　　弟弟，　　<u>沒有</u>　　妹妹。

6. 　　　　妹妹，　　　　　　姐姐。

7. 　　　　姐姐，　　　　　　弟弟。

8. 　　　　女兒，　　　　　　兒子。

C. 有 (yǒu, there is/are)

1. Wǒ jiā　　　　　　yǒu　　liù　　ge rén.
2. Xiǎo Lǐ jiā　　　　　　sān
3. Zhāng lǎoshī jiā　　　　liǎng
4. Wáng xiānsheng jiā　　sì
5. Gāo xiǎojie jiā　　　　bā
6. Xiǎo Zhāng jiā　　　　wǔ

1. 我家　　　　有　　六　　個人。

2. 小李家　　　　　三

3. 張老師家　　　　兩

4. 王先生家　　　　四

5. 高小姐家　　　　八

6. 小張家　　　　　五

D. Question Pronouns 誰 (shéi, who), 幾個 (jǐge, how many), 什麼 (shénme, what). (Formulate a question for each of the sentences below using the appropriate question pronoun.)

Example: A: <u>Zhè shì shéi?</u>　　　　B: Zhè shì wǒ bàba.

A：<u>這是誰？</u>　　　　B：這是我爸爸。

1. A: _____?　　B: Nà shì wǒ jiějie.
2. A: _____?　　B: Xiǎo Zhāng jiā yǒu liù ge rén.
3. A: _____?　　B: Xiǎo Gāo yǒu sān ge jiějie.
4. A: _____?　　B: Wǒ bàba shì lǜshī.
5. A: _____?　　B: Wǒ yǒu liǎngge Zhōngguó lǎoshī.
6. A: _____?　　B: Tā gēge shì yīshēng.
7. A: _____?　　B: Tā jiào Zhāng Yǒuzhōng.

1. A：＿＿＿＿＿＿＿＿＿？   B：那是我姐姐。

2. A：＿＿＿＿＿＿＿＿＿？   B：小張家有六個人。

3. A：＿＿＿＿＿＿＿＿＿？   B：小高有三個姐姐。

4. A：＿＿＿＿＿＿＿＿＿？   B：我爸爸是律師。

5. A：＿＿＿＿＿＿＿＿＿？   B：我有兩個中國老師。

6. A：＿＿＿＿＿＿＿＿＿？   B：他哥哥是醫生。

7. A：＿＿＿＿＿＿＿＿＿？   B：他叫張有中。

E. 都 (dōu, both, all) (Rephrase the sentences by using 都 .)

Example: Wǒ bàba shì yīshēng, tā bàba yě shì yīshēng.
       ---->   Wǒ bàba hé tā bàba dōu shì yīshēng.

我爸爸是醫生，他爸爸也是醫生。

-->我爸爸和他爸爸都是醫生。

1. Wǒ gēge shì lǜshī, wǒ jiějie yě shì lǜshī. ---->
2. Wáng Péng shì xuésheng, Lǐ Yǒu yě shì xuésheng. ---->
3. Wǒ bàba shì lǎoshī, tā bàba yě shì lǎoshī. ---->
4. Wǒ jiā yǒu sān ge rén, Xiǎo Zhāng jiā yě yǒu sān ge rén. ---->
5. Wǒ yǒu liǎng ge dìdi, tā yě yǒu liǎng ge dìdi. ---->
6. Zhège xuésheng shì Zhōngguórén, nàge xuésheng yě shì Zhōngguórén. --->
7. Zhè zhāng zhàopiàn shì nǐ de, nà zhāng zhàopiàn yě shì nǐ de. ---->
8. Wǒ māma xìng Gāo, tā māma yě xìng Gāo. ---->

1. 我哥哥是律師，我姐姐也是律師。   --->

2. 王朋是學生，李友也是學生。   --->

3. 我爸爸是老師，他爸爸也是老師。   --->

4. 我家有三個人，小張家也有三個人。---->

5. 我有兩個弟弟，他也有兩個弟弟。   --->

6. 這個學生是中國人，那個學生也是中國人。---->

7. 這張照片是你的，那張照片也是你的。---->

8. 我媽媽姓高，他媽媽也姓高。---->

F. 都 (dōu, all, both) with 不 (bù, not) or 沒有 (méiyǒu, have not)

Examples:
(1) Wáng Zhōng shì lǎoshī. Lǐ Shēng shì lǎoshī. Gāo Péng shì yīshēng. (lǜshī)
   ---> Wáng Zhōng, Lǐ Shēng, Gāo Péng dōu bú shì lǜshī.

(2) Xiǎo Zhāng méiyǒu gēge. Xiǎo Lǐ méiyǒu gēge. Xiǎo Wáng yě méiyǒu gēge.
   ---> Xiǎo Zhāng, Xiǎo Lǐ, Xiǎo Wáng dōu méiyǒu gēge.

(1) 王中是老師。李生是老師。高朋是醫生。（律師）

   --> 王中、李生、高朋都不是律師。

(2) 小張沒有哥哥。小李沒有哥哥。小王也沒有哥哥。

   --> 小張、小李、小王都沒有哥哥。

1. Wǒ bàba shì lǎoshī. Wǒ jiějie shì lǜshī. Wǒ gēge shì yīshēng. (xuésheng)
2. Xiǎo Wáng méiyǒu mèimei. Xiǎo Lǐ méiyǒu mèimei. Xiǎo Zhāng yě méiyǒu mèimei. (mèimei)
3. Wáng Zhōng shì Měiguórén. Lǐ Yǒu shì Měiguórén. Gāo Guì shì Měiguórén. (Zhōngguórén)
4. Lǐ Zhōng shì lǎoshī. Wáng Péng bú shì lǎoshī. Gāo Yǒu yě bú shì lǎoshī. (lǎoshī)
5. Wáng Péng méiyǒu zhàopiàn. Lǐ Zhōng méiyǒu zhàopiàn. Gāo Yǒu méiyǒu zhàopiàn. (zhàopiàn)
6. Wǒ māma xìng Wáng. Nǐ māma xìng Gāo. Tā bàba xìng Zhāng. (Lǐ)

1. 我爸爸是老師，我姐姐是律師，我哥哥是醫生。（學生）
2. 小王沒有妹妹，小李沒有妹妹，小張也沒有妹妹。
（妹妹）
3. 王中是美國人，李友是美國人，高貴是美國人。
（中國人）
4. 李中是老師，王朋不是老師，高友也不是老師。（老師）
5. 王朋沒有照片，李中沒有照片，高友沒有照片。（照片）
6. 我媽媽姓王，你媽媽姓高，她爸爸姓張。（李）

PRONUNCIATION EXERCISES

A. Practice the following initials:

1. zh   ch   sh
    zhè   chè   shè
    zhǎo   chǎo   shǎo
    zhāng   chàng   shāng
    zhuāng   chuáng   shuāng

2. d   dà   duō   duì   dōu
    t   tà   tuō   tuì   tōu

3. r   rén   rào   rì   rè

B. Practice the final "e":

    gē   dé   zhè   hē
    kē   tè   chē   shé
    zé   cè   sè   rè

C. Practice the following tones:

    chénggōng   chángcháng   rénkǒu   xuéxiào
    Chángjiāng Chángchéng   míngxiǎn   chídào

D. Practice the following syllables with neutral tone:

    māma   shéi de   jiějie   mèimei
    tā de   fángzi   nǐ de   dìdi

ENGLISH TEXT

Dialogue I

(Wang Peng is in Little Gao's room pointing to a picture on the wall.)

Wang Peng:　　Little Gao, is that picture yours?

(They both walk toward the picture and then stand in front of it.)

Little Gao:　　Yes. This is my dad. This is my mom.
Wang Peng:　　Who is this boy?
Little Gao:　　This is my younger brother.
Wang Peng:　　Is this girl your younger sister?
Little Gao:　　No, she is Mr. Li's daughter.
Wang Peng:　　Does Mr. Li have any sons?
Little Gao:　　He has no sons.

Dialogue II

Li You: Little Zhang, how many people are there in your family?

Little Zhang: There are six people in my family: my dad, my mom, an older brother, two older sisters and I. How many people are there in your family, Miss Li?

Li You: There are five people in my family: my dad, my mom, my two younger sisters and I. What do your dad and mom do?

Little Zhang: My mom is an English teacher. My dad is a lawyer. My older brother and sisters are all college students.

Li You: My mom is also a teacher. My dad is a doctor.

Lesson Three   Dates and Time
第三課   時間

DIALOGUE I: *TAKING SOMEONE OUT TO EAT ON HIS/HER BIRTHDAY*

Vocabulary

1.	九月	jiǔyuè	N	September
	月	yuè	N	month
2.	十二	shí'èr	Nu	twelve
3.	號	hào	N	day of the month; number
4.	星期四	xīngqīsì	N	Thursday
	星期	xīngqī	N	week
5.	天	tiān	N	day
6.	生日	shēngrì	N	birthday

	生	shēng	V	to give birth to; to be born
	日	rì	N	day; sun
7.	今年	jīnnián	T	this year
	年	nián	N	year
8.	多大	duō dà	CE	how old
	多	duō	Adv	how many/much; to what extent
	大	dà	Adj	big; old
9.	十八	shíbā	Nu	eighteen
10.	歲	suì	N	year (of age)
11.	請	qǐng	V	to treat (somebody); to invite [See also L.1]
12.	吃	chī	V	to eat
13.	晚飯	wǎnfàn	N	dinner; supper
	晚	wǎn	N/Adj	evening; night; late
	飯	fàn	N	meal; (cooked) rice
14.	吃飯	chī fàn	VO	to eat (a meal)
15.	怎麼樣	zěnmeyàng	QPr	How does it sound? Is it O.K.?
16.	太…了	tài…le		too; extremely
17.	謝謝	xièxie	CE	thank you
18.	喜歡	xǐhuan	V	to like; to prefer
19.	還是	háishi	Conj	or
20.	可是	kěshì	Conj	but
21.	好	hǎo	Adj	O.K.

23.	我們	wǒmen	Pr	we
24.	點鐘	diǎnzhōng	N	o'clock
	點	diǎn	N	o'clock
	鐘	zhōng	N	clock
25.	半	bàn	Nu	half; half an hour
26.	晚上	wǎnshang	T	evening; night
27.	見	jiàn	V	to see
28.	再見	zàijiàn	CE	good-bye; see you again
	再	zài	Adv	again

Proper Noun

29.	小白	Xiǎo Bái		Little Bai
	白	bái	Adj	(a surname); white

九 月						
日	一	二	三	四	五	六
1	2	3	4	5	6	7
8	9	10	11	12	13	14
15	16	17	18	19	20	21
22	23	24	25	26	27	28
29	30					

Dialogue I: *Pinyin*

(Little Gao is talking to Little Bai.)

Xiǎo Gāo: Xiǎo Bái, jiǔyuè <u>shí'èr</u> (G1) <u>hào</u> (G2) shì <u>xīngqī jǐ</u> (G2)?

Xiǎo Bái: Shì xīngqīsì.

Xiǎo Gāo: Nà tiān shì wǒ <u>de</u> (G3) shēngrì.

Xiǎo Bái: Shì ma? Nǐ jīnnián duō dà (1)?

Xiǎo Gāo: Shíbā suì.

Xiǎo Bái: Xīngqīsì <u>wǒ qǐng nǐ chī wǎnfàn</u> (G4), zěnmeyàng?

Xiǎo Gāo: Tài hǎo le. Xièxie, xièxie (2).

Xiǎo Bái: Nǐ xǐhuan chī Zhōngguófàn <u>háishi</u> (G5) Měiguófàn?

Xiǎo Gāo: Wǒ shì Zhōngguórén, kěshì wǒ xǐhuan chī Měiguófàn.

Xiǎo Bái: Hǎo, wǒmen chī Měiguó fàn.

Xiǎo Gāo: Xīngqīsì jǐ diǎnzhōng?

Xiǎo Bái: Qīdiǎn bàn zěnmeyàng?

Xiǎo Gāo: Hǎo, xīngqīsì wǎnshang jiàn.

Xiao Bai: Zàijiàn.

Dialogue I: *Chinese*

(Little Gao is talking to Little Bai.)

小高：小白，九月<u>十二</u>^(G1)號^(G2)是<u>星期幾</u>^(G2)？

小白：是星期四。

小高：那天是我<u>的</u>^(G3)生日。

小白：是嗎？你今年多大⁽¹⁾？

小高：十八歲。

小白：星期四<u>我請你吃晚飯</u>^(G4)，怎麼樣？

小高：太好了。謝謝，謝謝⁽²⁾。

小白：你喜歡吃中國飯<u>還是</u>^(G5)美國飯？

小高：我是中國人，可是我喜歡吃美國飯。

小白：好，我們吃美國飯。

小高：星期四幾點鐘？

小白：<u>七點半</u>^(G2)怎麼樣？

小高：好，星期四晚上見。

小白：再見！

Notes:

(1) When inquiring about someone's age, say 幾歲 (jǐ suì) or 多大 (duō dà) if the person is under ten. Otherwise say 多大 (duō dà). If it is an old person, one can say 您多大年紀/歲數 (niánjì/suìshù, age) 了？(Nín duō dà niánjì/suìshù le?)

(2) To show gratitude, one can say "謝謝" (xièxie), or "謝謝，謝謝" (xièxie, xièxie) by repeating the word. The latter one is obviously more polite and exuberant.

Dialogue II: *Inviting Someone to Dinner*

Vocabulary

1.	現在	xiànzài	T	now
2.	刻	kè	T	quarter (hour); 15 minutes
3.	事	shì	N	matter; affair; business
4.	明天	míngtiān	T	tomorrow
5.	忙	máng	Adj	busy
6.	今天	jīntiān	T	today
7.	很	hěn	Adv	very
8.	為什麼	wèishénme	QPr	why
	為（爲）**	wèi	Prep	for
9.	因爲	yīnwèi	Conj	because
10.	還有	háiyǒu		in addition; also
11.	同學	tóngxué	N	classmate
12.	認識	rènshi	V	to know (someone); to recognize

Proper Nouns

13.	小李	Xiǎo Lǐ		Little Li

** Please note that the character **wèi** (for) appears in two forms. "爲" is the printing form, and "為" is the hand-written form.

Dialogue II: *Pinyin*

(Wang Peng and Little Bai are talking to each other.)

Wáng Péng: Xiǎo Bái, xiànzài jǐ diǎnzhōng?

Xiǎo Bái: Wǔ diǎn sān kè.

Wáng Péng: Wǒ liù diǎn yí kè yǒu shì.

Xiǎo Bái: Wáng Péng, nǐ míngtiān <u>máng bu máng</u> ^(G6)?

Wáng Péng: Wǒ jīntiān hěn máng, kěshì míngtiān bù máng. Yǒu shì ma?

Xiǎo Bái: Míngtian wǒ qǐng nǐ chī wǎnfàn, zěnmeyàng?

Wáng Péng: Wèishénme qǐng wǒ chī wǎnfàn?

Xiǎo Bái: Yīnwèi míngtiān shì Xiǎo Gāo de shēngrì.

Wáng Péng: Shì ma? Hǎo, <u>háiyǒu</u> ^(G7) shéi?

Xiǎo Bái: Hái yǒu wǒ de tóngxué Xiǎo Lǐ.

Wáng Péng: Nà tài hǎo le! Wǒ yě rènshi Xiǎo Lǐ. Jǐ diǎnzhōng?

Xiǎo Bái: Míngtiān wǎnshang qī diǎn bàn.

Wáng Péng: Hǎo, míngtiān qī diǎn bàn jiàn.

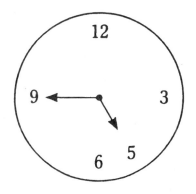
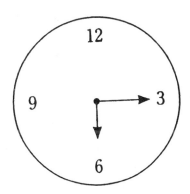

Can you say the times in the pictures above in Chinese?

Dialogue II: *Chinese*

(Wang Peng and Little Bai are talking to each other.)

王朋： 小白，現在幾點鐘？

小白： 五點三刻。

王朋： 我六點一刻有事。

小白： 王朋，你明天<u>忙不忙</u>(G6)？

王朋： 我今天很忙，可是明天不忙。有事嗎？

小白： 明天我請你吃晚飯，怎麼樣？

王朋： 為什麼請我吃飯？

小白： 因為明天是小高的生日。

王朋： 是嗎？好。<u>還有</u>(G7)誰？

小白： 還有我的同學小李。

王朋： 那太好了，我也認識小李。幾點鐘？

小白： 明天晚上七點半。

王朋： 好，明天七點半見。

On Birthdays in China

The Chinese equivalent of a birthday cake is noodles. Because noodles are long, they are considered a symbol of longevity. That is why they are called 長壽麵 (chángshòu miàn, longevity noodles). Among the younger generations in urban areas birthday cakes are also becoming quite common.

Supplementary Vocabulary

1. 分	fēn	N	minute
2. 差	chà	V	to be short of; lack
3. 昨天	zuótiān	T	yesterday
4. 前天	qiántiān	T	the day before yesterday
5. 後天	hòutiān	T	the day after tomorrow
6. 明年	míngnián	T	next year
7. 去年	qùnián	T	last year
8. 前年	qiánnián	T	the year before last
9. 後年	hòunián	T	the year after next
10. 下(個)月	xià(ge)yuè	T	next month
11. 錶	biǎo	N	watch

Year and Day Compared

大前天	前天	昨天	今天	明天	後天	大後天
大前年	前年	去年	今年	明年	後年	大後年

Please note that the above expressions referring to 天 "tiān" (day) and 年 "nián" (year) parallel each other except for 昨天 "zuótiān" (yesterday) and 去年 "qùnián" (last year).

Month and Week Compared

上上個月	上個月	這個月	下個月	下下個月
上上個星期	上個星期	這個星期	下個星期	下下個星期

Please note that the above expressions referring to 月 "yuè" (month) and 星期 "xīngqī" (week) parallel each other. The measure word 個 "gè" can be omitted.

GRAMMAR

1. Numbers (0, 11-100)

0: 零 (líng, zero)

11-99: 十一 (shíyī, eleven), 十二 (shí'èr, twelve),

十三 (shísān, thirteen)... 二十 (èrshí, twenty),

二十一 (èrshíyī, twenty-one), 二十二 (èrshí'èr, twenty-two),

二十三 (èrshísān, twenty-three)... 三十 (sānshí, thirty),

九十一 (jiǔshíyī, ninety-one)... 九十九 (jiǔshíjiǔ, ninety-nine).

100--: 一百 (yìbǎi, one hundred), 二百 (èrbǎi, two hundred).

2. Dates and Time

(1) <u>The days of the week:</u>

星期一	xīngqīyī	Monday
星期二	xīngqī'èr	Tuesday
星期三	xīngqīsān	Wednesday
星期四	xīngqīsì	Thursday
星期五	xīngqīwǔ	Friday
星期六	xīngqīliù	Saturday
星期日	xīngqīrì	Sunday

While 星期 (xīngqī, week) is commonly used in spoken Chinese, 週 (zhōu, week) is commonly used in written Chinese. Monday can also be called 週一 (zhōuyī), Tuesday 週二 (zhōu'èr), etc. Weekend is 週末 (zhōumò), and in Written Chinese 週日 (zhōurì) is sometimes used to refer to Sunday. In China, the week starts on Monday. The expression 星期幾? (xīngqī jǐ?) is used to find out the day of the week. To answer this question, simply replace the word 幾 (jǐ, what, how many) with the number indicating the day of the week, such as 星期四 (xīngqīsì, Thursday), meaning the fourth day of the week. In spoken Chinese the expression 禮拜 (lǐbài, week) is also used. Therefore, 禮拜四 also means Thursday.

(2) <u>The months of the year:</u>

一月	yīyuè	January
二月	èryuè	February
三月	sānyuè	March
四月	sìyuè	April
五月	wǔyuè	May
六月	liùyuè	June
七月	qīyuè	July
八月	bāyuè	August
九月	jiǔyuè	September
十月	shíyuè	October
十一月	shíyīyuè	November
十二月	shí'èryuè	December

(3) <u>The days of the month:</u>

In spoken Chinese, the word 號 (hào, number) is used to refer to the days of the month. However, in written Chinese the word 日 (rì, day) is always used.

Examples:

二月五號	èryuè wǔ hào	Feburary 5	(Spoken)
二月五日	èryuè wǔ rì	Feburary 5	(Written)

(4) <u>Year:</u>

In Chinese, the word 年 (nián, year) is always added to the numerals referring to a year.

Examples:

一七七六年	yī qī qī liù nián	1776
一九九五年	yī jiǔ jiǔ wǔ nián	1995

Note: In Chinese, years are read one number at a time, unlike in English, where one says "seventeen seventy-six" or "nineteen ninety-five."

(5) <u>Word order for dates:</u>

When giving dates in Chinese, the following order is used:

year	month	day	day of the week
年	月	日	星期
nián	yuè	rì	xīngqī

Examples:

一九九五年七月二十六日星期三 (Wednesday, July 26, 1995)

yī jiǔ jiǔ wǔ nián qīyuè èrshíliù rì xīngqīsān

(6) <u>Telling Time:</u>

These words are used to tell time in Chinese: 點鐘 (diǎnzhōng, o'clock), 半 (bàn, half hour), 刻 (kè, quarter hour), and 分 (fēn, minute).
Examples:

a. <u>o'clock:</u>

三點鐘	sān diǎnzhōng	three o'clock
十一點	shíyī diǎn	eleven o'clock
七、八點鐘	qī, bā diǎnzhōng	seven or eight o'clock

Note: 鐘 (zhōng) in 點鐘 (diǎnzhōng) can be omitted.

b. <u>minute:</u>

一點十八(分)	yī diǎn shíbā (fēn)	1:18	
兩點七(分)	liǎng diǎn qī (fēn)	2:07	
三點零五(分)	sān diǎn líng wǔ (fēn)	3:05	
五點二十(分)	wǔ diǎn èrshí(fēn)	5:20	
差十分九點	chà shí fēn jiǔ diǎn	8:50	(ten till nine)

Note: The word 分 (fēn, minute) can be omitted. The word 零 (líng, zero) can be added before the minute if it is a single digit number.

c. <u>quarter hour:</u>

    兩點一刻   liǎng diǎn yí kè   2:15   (quarter after two)

    差一刻四點   chà yí kè sì diǎn   3:45   (quarter of four)

    十一點三刻   shíyī diǎn sān kè   11:45

d. <u>half hour:</u>

    兩點半   liǎng diǎn bàn   2:30   (half past two)

    八點半   bā diǎn bàn   8:30   (half past eight)

    十二點半   shí'èr diǎn bàn   12:30   (half past twelve)

e. <u>evening time:</u>

    晚上七點(鐘)   wǎnshang qī diǎn(zhōng)   7:00 p.m.

    晚上八點零五(分)   wǎnshang bā diǎn líng wǔ (fēn)   8:05 p.m.

    晚上九點一刻   wǎnshang jiǔ diǎn yí kè   9:15 p.m.

    晚上十點半   wǎnshang shí diǎn bàn   10:30 p.m.

    晚上差四分十一點 wǎnshang chà sì fēn shíyī diǎn   10:56 p.m.

3. Pronouns as Modifiers and the Usage of 的 (de)

When personal pronouns like 我 (wǒ, I), 你 (nǐ, you), and 他 (tā, he) are followed by forms of address such as 媽媽 (māma, mother), 弟弟 (dìdi, younger brother), and 老師 (lǎoshī, teacher) the word 的 (de) can be omitted; e.g., 我媽媽 (wǒ māma, my mother), 你弟弟 (nǐ dìdi, your younger brother), 我們老師 (wǒmen lǎoshī, our teacher). Otherwise 的 (de) is generally required; e.g., 我的生日 (wǒ de shēngrì, my birthday).

4. Pivotal Sentences

In this sentence "我請你吃晚飯." (Wǒ qǐng nǐ chī wǎnfàn. I will treat you to dinner.), 你 (nǐ, you) is the object of the verb 請 (qǐng, to treat). At the same time it is the subject of the verb 吃 (chī, to eat).

Examples:

(1) 明天李生請你吃中國飯。

Míngtiān Lǐ Shēng qǐng nǐ chī Zhōngguófàn.

(Li Sheng is inviting you to eat Chinese food tomorrow.)

(2) 今天晚上我請你和你妹妹吃美國飯，好嗎？

Jīntiān wǎnshang wǒ qǐng nǐ hé nǐ mèimei chī Měiguófàn, hǎo ma?

(How about if I invite you and your younger sister to eat American food tonight?)

5. Alternative Questions

The structure (是)... 還是... (shì... háishi..., ...or...) is used to form an alternative question. If there is another verb used in the predicate, the first 是 (shì) can be omitted.

(1) 你是中國人，還是美國人？

Nǐ shì Zhōngguórén, háishi Měiguórén?

(Are you Chinese or American?)

(2) 你哥哥是老師，還是學生？

Nǐ gēge shì lǎoshī, háishi xuésheng?

(Is your older brother a teacher or a student?)

(3) 是你請我吃飯，還是他請我吃飯？

Shì nǐ qǐng wǒ chīfàn, háishi tā qǐng wǒ chīfàn?

(Who is taking me to dinner, you or he?)

(4) A: 他喜歡吃中國飯，還是喜歡吃美國飯？

Tā xǐhuan chī Zhōngguófàn, háishi xǐhuan chī Měiguófàn?

(Does he like to eat Chinese or American food?)

B: 中國飯美國飯他都喜歡。

Zhōngguó fàn Měiguó fàn tā dōu xǐhuan.

(He likes both Chinese food and American food.)

6. Affirmative + Negative (A-not-A) Questions (I)

In a sentence, if the affirmative form of the verb or the adjective is followed by the negative form of the same verb or the same adjective, the sentence becomes an "affirmative + negative (or A-not-A) question." Different from questions ending with 嗎 (ma) or 吧 (ba), an affirmative + negative question implies that the question is not leaning towards either the affirmative or negative side of the answer.

Example:

(1) 你忙不忙？

Nǐ máng bu máng?

(Are you busy?)

(2) 媽媽喜歡不喜歡吃中國飯？

Māma xǐhuan bu xǐhuan chī Zhōngguófàn?

(Does mother like to eat Chinese food?)

(3) 王太太今天有沒有事？

Wáng tàitai jīntiān yǒu méiyǒu shì?

(Does Mrs. Wang have anything to do today?)

7. 還有 (háiyǒu, also; too)

The word 還有 (hái) can signify addition. For instance,

(1) 我家有爸爸、媽媽，還有一個妹妹。

Wǒ jiā yǒu bàba, māma, hái yǒu yí ge mèimei.

(In my family, I have Dad, Mom, and a younger sister.)

(2) A: 誰喜歡吃美國飯？

Shéi xǐhuan chī Měiguó fàn?

(Who likes American food?)

B: 我，我弟弟，還有我姐姐。

Wǒ, wǒ dìdi, hái yǒu wǒ jiějie.

(Me, my younger brother, and also my older sister.)

PATTERN DRILLS

1. Days of the week (Provide the correct answers based on the calendar below.)

March						
Su	M	Tu	W	Th	F	Sa
12	13	14	15	16	17	18

Example:

   (Sānyuè shíwǔ hào)

A: Sānyuè shíwǔ hào shì xīngqī jǐ?

B: Sānyuè shíwǔ hào shì xīngqīsān.

（三月十五號）

A: 三月十五號是星期幾？

B: 三月十五號是星期三。

1. Sānyuè shísān hào
2. Sānyuè shíliù hào
3. Sānyuè shí'èr hào
4. Sānyuè shíqī hào
5. Sānyuè shíbā hào
6. Sānyuè shísì hào

1. 三月十三號

2. 三月十六號

3. 三月十二號

4. 三月十七號

5. 三月十八號

6. 三月十四號

2. Time

1. <u>Wǒmen</u>	wǔ diǎnzhōng	<u>jiàn</u>.
2.	liù diǎn èrshí fēn	
3.	jiǔ diǎn	
4.	qī diǎn bàn	
5.	bā diǎn shí fēn	
6.	shíyī diǎn sìshí fēn	

1. <u>我們</u>   五點鐘   見 。

2.   六點二十分

3.   九點

4.   七點半

5.   八點十分

6.   十一點四十分

3. 還是   (Form 還是 questions by using the given information.)

1. Tā shì xuésheng,	<u>háishi</u>	lǎoshī?
2. Xiǎo Gāo xǐhuan chī zhōngguófàn,		xǐhuan chī Měiguófàn?
3. Nǐ de lǎoshī xìng Gāo,		xìng Zhāng?
4. Nǐ jīnnián shì shíjiǔ,		èrshí?
5. Tā gēge shì yīshēng,		lǜshī?
6. Nǐ qǐng wǒ chīfàn,		wǒ qǐng nǐ chīfàn?

1. 他是學生   還是   老師？

2. 小高喜歡吃中國飯，   喜歡吃美國飯？

3. 你的老師姓高，   姓張？

4. 你今年是十九，   二十？

5. 他哥哥是醫生，   律師？

6. 你請我吃飯，   我請你吃飯？

4. <u>可是</u> (kěshì, but) (Rephrase the sentences by using 可是.)

Example: Xiǎo Gāo shì Zhōngguórén. Xiǎo Gāo xǐhuan chī Měiguófàn.
           ---> Xiǎo Gāo shì Zhōngguórén, <u>kěshì</u> tā xǐhuan chī Měiguófàn.

   小高是中國人。小高喜歡吃美國飯。

   --> 小高是中國人，<u>可是</u>他喜歡吃美國飯。

1. Wǒ xǐhuan Zhāng xiǎojie. Wǒ bù xǐhuan Bái xiǎojie.
2. Wǒ rènshi Wáng lǎoshī. Wǒ bú rènshi Lǐ lǎoshī.
3. Wǒ yǒu liǎng ge gēge. Wǒ méiyǒu dìdi.
4. Gāo lǜshī jīntiān hěn máng. Gāo lǜshī míngtiān bù máng.
5. Wǒ dìdi shì lǎoshī. Wǒ shì xuésheng.
6. Wǒ qǐng tā chīfàn. Tā bù qǐng wǒ chīfàn.

1. 我喜歡張小姐。我不喜歡白小姐。--->

2. 我認識王老師。我不認識李老師。--->

3. 我有兩個哥哥。我沒有弟弟。--->

4. 高律師今天很忙。高律師明天不忙。--->

5. 我弟弟是老師。我是學生。--->

6. 我請他吃飯。他不請我吃飯。--->

5.   Affirmative + Negative (A-not-A) Questions
     (Change the questions below into A not A questions.)

Example: Nǐ shì xuésheng ma?
              Nǐ shì bu shì xuésheng?

         你是學生嗎？

         --> 你是不是學生？

1. Tā gēge shì yīshēng ma? --->
2. Shíyuè wǔ hào shì xīngqīsì ma? --->
3. Nǐ qǐng wǒ chī wǎnfàn ma? --->
4. Gāo yīshēng xǐhuan chī Měiguófàn ma? --->
5. Wǒmen jīntiān wǎnshang chī Zhōngguófàn ma? --->
6. Zhāng lǎoshī jīntiān máng ma? --->
7. Wáng lǜshī rènshì Lǐ xiǎojie ma? --->
8. Xiǎo Bái shì nǐ de tóngxué ma? --->

1. 他哥哥<u>是</u>醫生嗎？ --->

2. 十月五號<u>是</u>星期四嗎？ --->

3. 你<u>請</u>我吃晚飯嗎？ --->

4. 高醫生<u>喜歡</u>吃美國飯嗎？ --->

5. 我們今天晚上<u>吃</u>中國飯嗎？ --->

6. 張老師今天<u>忙</u>嗎？ --->

7. 王律師<u>認識</u>李小姐嗎？ --->

8. 小白<u>是</u>你的同學嗎？ --->

6. <u>還有</u> (háiyǒu, also, in addition)

Examples: Nǐ rènshi shéi? (Wáng Péng, Xiǎo Gāo)
--->Wǒ rènshi Wáng Péng, háiyǒu Xiǎo Gāo.

你認識誰？（王朋，小高）

-->我認識王朋，<u>還有</u>小高。

1. Nǐ qǐng shéi chīfàn?	(Zhāng yīshēng, Lǐ lǎoshī, Bái lǜshī)
2. Nǐ xǐhuan chī shénme fàn?	(Měiguófàn, Zhōngguófàn)
3. Shéi qǐng nǐ chīfàn?	(Xiǎo Gāo, Xiǎo Lǐ, Xiǎo Wáng)
4. Shéi xǐhuan chī Zhōngguó fàn?	(Wǒ bàba, wǒ māma, wǒ dìdi)

1. 你請誰吃飯？ （張醫生、李老師、白律師）

2. 你喜歡吃什麼飯？ （美國飯，中國飯）

3. 誰請你吃飯？ （小高，小李，小王）

4. 誰喜歡吃中國飯？ （我爸爸，我媽媽，我弟弟）

PRONUNCIATION EXERCISES

A. The initial **r** :

shēngrì	rìjì	rèqíng	rénmín
réngrán	ránhòu	ruìlì	ràngbù

B. Finals:

1.   ie   jiè   xiě   dié   tiě
       ue   jué   xué   quē   qiē
2.   uo   duō   tuō   zuò   cuò
       ou   dōu   tóu   zǒu   còu
3.   u   dū   tū   zū   cū

C. Two-syllable words:

bàngōng	gànhuó	rìjì	xiànzài
dìqū	dìtú	dàxiě	jiàozhà

D. Neutral tone:

yī ge	sān ge	zhè ge	nà ge
tā de	shéi de	wǒ de	nǐ de

E. Tone sandhi:

zhǎnlǎn	lǚguǎn	yǔsǎn	děngděng
shǒufǎ	yǔnxǔ	xuǎnjǔ	guǎngchǎng

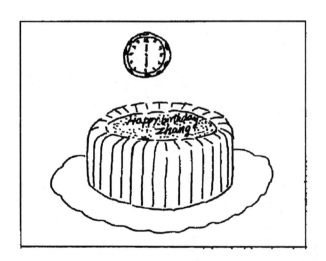

What occasion is this cake for?
What time is it?

ENGLISH TEXT

Dialogue I

Little Gao: Little Bai, what day is September 12?
Little Bai: It's a Thursday.
Little Gao: That day is my birthday.
Little Bai: Really? How old are you this year?
Little Gao: Eighteen.
Little Bai: I'll treat you to dinner on Thursday. How's that?
Little Gao: That would be great. Thank you very much!
Little Bai: Do you like Chinese food or American food?
Little Gao: I'm Chinese, but I like American food.
Little Bai: All right. Let's have American food.
Little Gao: Thursday what time?
Little Bai: How about seven-thirty?
Little Gao: All right. See you Thursday evening.
Little Bai: See you.

Dialogue II

Wang Peng: Xiao Bai, what time is it now?
Little Bai: Quarter to six.
Wang Peng: I have something to do at quarter after six.
Little Bai: Wang Peng, are you busy tomorrow?
Wang Peng: I'm very busy today, but I won't be tomorrow. What's up?
Little Bai: I'd like to take you to dinner tomorrow. What do you think?
Wang Peng: Why are you taking me to dinner?
Little Bai: Because tomorrow is Little Gao's birthday.
Wang Peng: Really? Great. (Are you taking) anyone else?
Little Bai: My classmate Little Li.
Wang Peng: That's fantastic. I know Little Li, too. What time?
Little Bai: Seven thirty tomorrow night.
Wang Peng: OK, I'll see you at seven thirty tomorrow.

Can you describe the picture below in Chinese?
Don't forget to mention the time.

Lesson Four   Hobbies
第四課　　愛好

DIALOGUE I: *ASKING ABOUT ONE'S HOBBIES*

Vocabulary

1.	週末	zhōumò	N	weekend
2.	打球	dǎ qiú	VO	to play ball
	打	dǎ	V	to hit; to strike
	球	qiú	N	ball
3.	看	kàn	V	to watch; to look
4.	電視	diànshì	N	TV
	電	diàn	N	electricity
	視	shì	N	vision

77

5. 唱歌	chàng gē	VO	to sing (a song)
唱	chàng	V	to sing
歌	gē	N	song
6. 跳舞	tiào wǔ	VO	to dance
跳	tiào	V	to jump
舞	wǔ	N	dance
7. 聽	tīng	V	to listen
8. 音樂	yīnyuè	N	music
9. 對	duì	Adj.	right; correct
10. 有時候	yǒu shíhou	CE	sometimes
時候	shíhou	N	(a point in) time; moment; (a duration of) time
11. 看書	kàn shū	VO	read books; read
書	shū	N	book
12. 電影	diànyǐng	N	movie
影	yǐng	N	shadow
13. 常常	chángcháng	Adv	often
14. 那	nà	Conj	in that case; then
15. 去	qù	V	to go
16. 外國	wàiguó	N	foreign country
17. 請客	qǐng kè	VO	to invite someone to dinner; to play the host
18. 昨天	zuótiān	T	yesterday
19. 所以	suǒyǐ	Conj	so

Dialogue I: *Pinyin*

(Little Bai is talking to Little Gao.)

Xiǎo Bái: Xiǎo Gāo, nǐ zhōumò xǐhuan zuò shénme?

Xiǎo Gāo: Wǒ xǐhuan dǎqiú, kàn diànshì. Nǐ ne?

Xiǎo Bái: Wǒ xǐhuan chànggē, tiàowǔ, hái xǐhuan tīng yīnyuè.

Xiǎo Gāo: Nǐ yě xǐhuan kànshū, duì bu duì?

Xiǎo Bái: Duì, yǒu shíhou yě xǐhuan kàn shū.

Xiǎo Gāo: Nǐ <u>xǐhuan bu xǐhuan</u> (G1) kàn diànyǐng?

Xiǎo Bái: Xǐhuan. <u>Wǒ zhōumò chángcháng kàn diànyǐng</u> (G2).

Xiǎo Gāo: <u>Nà</u> (G3) wǒmen jīntiān wǎnshang <u>qù kàn</u> (G4) yí ge wàiguó diànyǐng,
              zěnmeyàng?

Xiǎo Bái: Hǎo. Jīntiān wǒ qǐngkè.

Xiǎo Gāo: Wèishénme nǐ qǐngkè?

Xiǎo Bái: Yīnwei zuótiān nǐ qǐng wǒ chīfàn, suǒyǐ jīntiān wǒ qǐng nǐ kàn
              diànyǐng.

Do you do the following things on weekends? What do you do often?

Dialogue I: *Chinese*

(Little Bai is talking to Little Gao.)

小白：小高，你週末喜歡做什麼？

小高：我喜歡打球、看電視。你呢？

小白：我喜歡唱歌、跳舞，還喜歡聽音樂。

小高：你也喜歡看書，對不對？

小白：對，有時候也喜歡看書。

小高：你喜歡不喜歡^(G1)看電影？

小白：喜歡。我週末常常看電影^(G2)。

小高：那^(G3)我們今天晚上去看^(G4)一個外國電影，怎麼樣？

小白：好。今天我請客。

小高：為什麼你請客？

小白：因為昨天你請我吃飯，所以今天我請你看電影。

Dialogue II: *Inviting Someone to Play Ball*

Vocabulary

1. 好久	hǎojiǔ	CE	a long time
久	jiǔ	Adj	for a long time
2. 不錯	búcuò	Adj	not bad; pretty good
錯	cuò	Adj	wrong
3. 想	xiǎng	AV	to want to; to think

4. 覺得	juéde	V	to feel
5. 有意思	yǒu yìsi	CE	interesting
意思	yìsi	N	meaning
6. 只	zhǐ	Adv	only
7. 睡覺	shuì jiào	VO	to sleep
睡	shuì	V	to sleep
8. 算了	suàn le	CE	Forget it. Never mind.
9. 找	zhǎo	V	to look for
10. 別(的)	bié (de)	Adv	other

Dialogue II: *Pinyin*

(Wang Peng is talking to Xiao Zhang.)

Wáng Péng: Xiǎo Zhāng, hǎo jiǔ bú jiàn, nǐ hǎo ma?

Xiǎo Zhāng: Wǒ hěn hǎo. Nǐ zěnmeyàng?

Wáng Péng: Wǒ yě búcuò. Zhège zhōumò nǐ xiǎng (G5) zuò shénme?

Xiǎng bu xiǎng qù dǎqiú?

Xiǎo Zhāng: Dǎqiú? Wǒ bù xǐhuan dǎqiú.

Wáng Péng: Nà wǒmen qù kàn diànyǐng, hǎo ma (G6)?

Xiǎo Zhāng: Kàn diànyǐng? Wǒ juéde kàn diànyǐng yě méiyǒu yìsi.

Wáng Péng: Nà nǐ xǐhuan zuò shénme?

Xiǎo Zhāng: Wǒ zhǐ xǐhuan chīfàn, shuìjiào.

Wáng Péng: Nà suàn le. Wǒ qù zhǎo bié rén.

Which one do you like better?

(Please give your answer in Chinese.)

Dialogue II: *Chinese*

(Wang Peng is talking to Little Zhang.)

王朋：小張，好久不見，你好嗎？

小張：我很好。你怎麼樣？

王朋：我也不錯。這個週末你想^(G5)做什麼？想不
　　　想去打球？

小張：打球？我不喜歡打球。

王朋：那我們去看電影，好嗎^(G6)？

小張：看電影？我覺得看電影也沒有意思。

王朋：那你喜歡做什麼？

小張：我只喜歡吃飯、睡覺。

王朋：那算了。我去找別人。

Supplementary Vocabulary

1.	對了	duì le	CE	That's right!
2.	籃球	lánqiú	N	basketball
3.	網球	wǎngqiú	N	tennis
4.	橄欖球	gǎnlǎnqiú	N	football
5.	棒球	bàngqiú	N	baseball
6.	足球	zúqiú	N	soccer
7.	排球	páiqiú	N	volleyball

GRAMMAR

1. Affirmative + Negative Questions (II)

In this type of question there can be no adverbials before the verb except for time words. If there is an adverbial (such as 很 {hěn, very}, 都 {dōu, all}, and 常常 {chángcháng, often}) before the verb, the 嗎 type question must be used instead.

(1) 你明天去不去？

Nǐ míngtiān qù bu qù?

(Are you going tomorrow?)

(2) 她今天晚上看不看電視？

Tā jīntiān wǎnshang kàn bu kàn diànshì?

(Is she going to watch T.V. tonight?)

(3) 他們都是學生嗎？

Tāmen dōu shì xuésheng ma?

(Are they all students?)

(3a) **Incorrect:** 他們都是不是學生？

Tāmen dōu shì bu shì xuésheng?

(4) 你常常看電影嗎？

Nǐ chángcháng kàn diànyǐng ma?

(Do you often go to the movies?)

(4a) **Incorrect:** 你常常看不看電影？

Nǐ chángcháng kàn bu kàn diànyǐng?

(5) 張醫生很忙嗎？

Zhāng yīshēng hěn máng ma?

(Is Dr. Zhang very busy?)

(5a) **Incorrect:** 張醫生很忙不忙？

Zhāng yīshēng hěn máng bu máng?

2. Word Order in Chinese

The basic word order in a Chinese sentence goes like this:

Subj. + Adverbial + Verb + Obj.

Subject (agent of the action) + Adverbial (time, place, manner, etc.) + Verb + Object (receiver of the action)

Examples: Subject   Adv. of time   Verb   Object

(1) 他   今天   吃   中國飯。

Tā   jīntiān   chī   Zhōngguófàn.

(He is eating Chinese food today.)

(2) 我   週末常常   看   電影。

Wǒ zhōumò chángcháng kàn diànyǐng.

(I often watch movies on weekends.)

This is the most common word order in a Chinese sentence. (Please also see Grammar Note 2 in Lesson Two.) Of course, we will learn of particular situations in which the word order may deviate from the norm.

3. 那（麼）(Nà {me}) as a Cohesive Device

那（麼）(Nà {me}) can function as a cohesive device in a dialogue.

For example:

(1) 你今天晚上不想打球，那麼我們去看一個外國
電影，怎麼樣？

Nǐ jīntiān wǎnshang bù xiǎng dǎ qiú, nàme wǒmen qù kàn yí gè wàiguó diànyǐng, zěnmeyàng?

(You don't feel like playing ball this evening. Then let's go and see a foreign movie. How is that?)

(2) A: 我今天很忙，不想去吃晚飯。

Wǒ jīntiān hěn máng, bù xiǎng qù chī wǎnfàn.

(I'm very busy today. I don't want to go to dinner.)

B: 那明天呢？

　　Nà míngtiān ne?

　　(How about tomorrow?)

(3) A: 你喜歡不喜歡吃美國飯？

　　Nǐ xǐhuan bu xǐhuan chī Měiguó fàn?

　　(Do you like to eat American food?)

B: 不喜歡。

　　Bù xǐhuan.

　　(No, I don't.)

A: 那我們吃中國飯，怎麼樣？

　　Nà wǒmen chī Zhōngguó fàn, zěnmeyàng?

　　(Then let's eat Chinese food. How do you like that?)

B: 我也不喜歡。

　　Wǒ yě bù xǐhuan.

　　(I don't like that either.)

4. 去 (qù, to go) + V

　　To indicate that the performance of an action involves moving away from where the speaker is, the 去 (qù) + V construction must be used.
For example:

(1) 我們去看電影。

　　Wǒmen qù kàn diànyǐng.

　　(We are going to see a movie.)

(2) 晚上我不去跳舞。

　　Wǎnshang wǒ bú qù tiào wǔ.

　　(I will not go dancing tonight.)

(3) 今天我想去打球，你覺得怎麼樣？

　　Jīntiān wǒ xiǎng qù dǎ qiú, nǐ juéde zěnmeyàng?

　　(I would like to play ball today. What do you think?)

5. The Auxiliary Verb 想 (xiǎng, to want to)

想 (xiǎng) has several meanings. In this lesson 想 (xiǎng) is a modal verb. It indicates a desire to do something. It must be followed by a verb or sentence. For example:

(1) 你想聽音樂嗎？

Nǐ xiǎng tīng yīnyuè ma?

(Do you want to listen to some music?)

(2) 今天白老師想打球，可是王老師不想打。

Jīntiān Bái lǎoshī xiǎng dǎ qiú, kěshì Wáng lǎoshī bù xiǎng dǎ.

(Today Teacher Bai felt like playing ball, but Teacher Wang didn't.)

The interrogative form is 想不想(xiǎng bu xiǎng).

(3) 你想不想看中國電影？

Nǐ xiǎng bu xiǎng kàn Zhōngguó diànyǐng?

(Do you feel like going to see a Chinese movie?)

(4) 你想不想聽外國音樂？

Nǐ xiǎng bu xiǎng tīng wàiguó yīnyuè?

(Do you feel like listening to some foreign music?)

6. Questions with 好嗎 (hǎo ma)

To inquire about someone's opinion in a polite way, one can use好嗎 (hǎo ma). For example:

(1) 我們去看電影，好嗎？

Wǒmen qù kàn diànyǐng, hǎo ma?

(Let's go see a movie, all right?)

(2) 我們今天晚上吃中國飯，好嗎？

Wǒmen jīntiān wǎnshang chī Zhōngguófàn, hǎo ma?

(We will eat Chinese food tonight, all right?)

PATTERN DRILLS

A. Sub + Time + V + (Obj)

1. Tā dìdi	zhōumò chángcháng	dǎ qiú.
2. Wángpéng, Lǐyǒu		kàn Zhōngguó diànyǐng.
3. Gāo lǎoshī		qǐng xuésheng chī fàn.
4. Wǒ jiějie		tiào wǔ.
5. Xiǎo Wáng		kàn diànshì.
6. Bái xiǎojie		tīng yīnyuè.

1. 她弟弟　　　　　週末常常　　　　打球。

2. 王朋、李友　　　　　　　　　　看中國電影。

3. 高老師　　　　　　　　　　　　請學生吃飯。

4. 我姐姐　　　　　　　　　　　　跳舞。

5. 小王　　　　　　　　　　　　　看電視。

6. 白小姐　　　　　　　　　　　　聽音樂。

B. 去 + V

1. Wǒmen jīntiān wǎnshang	qù	tiào wǔ.
2.		chàng gē.
3.		dǎ qiú.
4.		kàn wàiguó diànyǐng.
5.		chī Měiguófàn.
6.		tīng Zhōngguó yīnyuè.

1. 我們今天晚上　　　去　　　跳舞。

2. 　　　　　　　　　　　　　唱歌。

3. 　　　　　　　　　　　　　打球。

4. 　　　　　　　　　　　　　看外國電影。

5. 　　　　　　　　　　　　　吃美國飯。

6. 　　　　　　　　　　　　　聽中國音樂。

C. 因為...所以...   (yīnwèi … suǒyǐ..., because...therefore...)

(Make sentences using 因為...所以...{yīnwèi … suǒyǐ...}.)

1. <u>Yīnwèi</u>	tā shì Zhōngguórén,	<u>suǒyǐ</u>	tā hěn xǐhuan chī Zhōngguófàn.
2.	tā hěn máng,		tā bú qù kàn diànyǐng.
3.	tā juéde dǎqiú méiyǒu yìsi,		tā bù xiǎng qù dǎ qiú,
4.	jīntiān de diànshì méiyǒu yìsi,		tā xiǎng qù kàn diànyǐng.
5.	tā xiǎng qù tiàowǔ,		tā bú qù kàn diànyǐng.
6.	tā juéde tīng yīnyuè méiyǒu yìsi,		tā bù tīng yīnyuè.

1. <u>因為</u>   他是中國人，   <u>所以</u>   他很喜歡吃中國飯。

2.   他很忙，   他不去看電影。

3.   他覺得打球沒有意思，   他不想去打球。

4.   今天的電視沒有意思，   他想去看電影。

5.   他想去跳舞，   他不去看電影。

6.   他覺得聽音樂沒有意思，   他不聽音樂。

D. 想   (xiǎng, want to)

1. Nǐ	<u>xiǎng bu xiǎng</u>	qù dǎ qiú?
2. Tā		chī Zhōngguófàn?
3. Gāo yīshēng		qù tiào wǔ?
4. Xiǎo Zhāng de mèimei		tīng yīnyuè?
5. Lǐ xiǎojie		qù kàn Měiguó diànyǐng?
6. Nǐmen		tīng yīnyuè?
7. Xiǎo Wáng de dìdi		kàn diànshì?

1. 你   <u>想不想</u>   去打球？

2. 他   吃中國飯？

3. 高醫生   去跳舞？

4. 小張的妹妹   聽音樂？

5. 李小姐   去看美國電影？

6. 你們   聽音樂？

7. 小王的弟弟   看電視？

E. 有意思 (yǒu yìsi, interesting)

1. Xiǎo Zhāng	juéde	dǎ qiú	hěn yǒu yìsi.
2. Bái yīshēng		tiào wǔ.	
3. Zhāng lǜshī		tīng Zhōngguó yīnyuè	
4. Lǐ lǎoshī		kàn wàiguó diànyǐng	
5. Wáng xiǎojie		kàn shū	
6. Xiǎo Gāo de dìdi		kàn diànshì	

1. 小張　　　　覺得　　打球　　　　　很有意思。

2. 白醫生　　　　　　跳舞

3. 張律師　　　　　　聽中國音樂

4. 李老師　　　　　　看外國電影

5. 王小姐　　　　　　看書

6. 小高的弟弟　　　　看電視

F. 好嗎？(hǎo ma? O.K.?)

1. Wǒmen	zhège zhōumò	qù	kàn diànyǐng	hǎo ma?
2.	míngtiān		tiào wǔ,	
3.	xīngqīsì		chàng gē,	
4.	zhège zhōumò		Gāo lǎoshī jiā,	
5.	xīngqīliù		dǎ qiú,	
6.	xīngqīwǔ		kàn wàiguó diànyǐng,	
7.	jīntiān wǎnshang		tīng yīnyuè,	

1. 我們　　這個週末　　去　　看電影，　　好嗎？

2. 　　　明天　　　　　　跳舞，

3. 　　　星期四　　　　　唱歌，

4. 　　　這個週末　　　　高老師家，

5. 　　　星期六　　　　　打球，

6. 　　　星期五　　　　　看外國電影，

7. 　　　今天晚上　　　　聽音樂

ENGLISH TEXT

Dialogue I

Little Bai:	What do you like to do on weekends?
Little Gao:	I like to play ball and watch TV. How about you?
Little Bai:	I like to sing, to dance, and also to listen to music.
Little Gao:	You like reading as well, right?
Little Bai:	Yes, sometimes I like reading, too.
Little Gao:	Do you like to watch movies?
Little Bai:	Yes, I do. I often watch movies on weekends.
Little Gao:	Then let's go see a foreign movie this evening. How about it?
Little Bai:	Fine. I will treat today.
Little Gao:	Why is it your treat?
Little Bai:	Because you treated me to dinner yesterday, so today I'm treating you to a movie.

Dialogue II

Wang Peng:	Little Zhang, long time no see. How are you?
Little Zhang:	Great. How about you?
Wang Peng:	I'm fine, too. What would you like to do this weekend? Do you want to play ball?
Little Zhang:	Play ball? I don't like playing ball.
Wang Peng:	Then let's go see a movie. How is that?
Little Zhang:	Watch a movie? I don't think seeing a movie would be much fun either.
Wang Peng:	Then what do you like to do?
Little Zhang:	I only like to eat and sleep.
Wang Peng:	Then forget it. I'll ask somebody else.

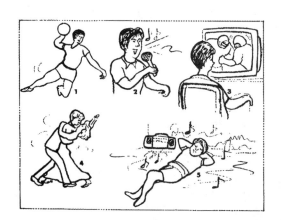

Please describe each of the ten pictures above.

Lesson Five   Visiting Friends
第五課   看朋友

DIALOGUE: *VISITING ONE'S HOME*

Vocabulary

1. 呀	ya	P	(used to soften a question)
2. 進	jìn	V	to enter
3. 快	kuài	Adj/Adv	fast; quick/quickly
4. 進來	jìnlai	VC	come in
5. 來	lái	V	to come
6. 介紹	jièshào	V	to introduce
7. 一下	yí xià	M	(used after a verb, indicating that the duration of the action

is short, or that one is trying out something; see G1)

8. 高興	gāoxìng	Adj	happy; pleased
9. 漂亮	piàoliang	Adj	pretty
10. 坐	zuò	V	to sit
11. 在	zài	Prep	at; in; on
12. 哪兒	nǎr	QPr	where
13. 工作	gōngzuò	V	to work
14. 學校	xuéxiào	N	school
15. 喝	hē	V	to drink
16. 點(兒)	diǎn(r)	M	a little; a bit; some
17. 茶	chá	N	tea
18. 咖啡	kāfēi	N	coffee
19. 啤酒	píjiǔ	N	beer
酒	jiǔ	N	wine
20. 吧	ba	P	(used to soften the tone)
21. 要	yào	V	to want; to have a desire for
22. 杯	bēi	M	cup; glass
23. 可樂	kělè	N	cola
24. 可以	kěyǐ	AV	can, may
25. 對不起	duìbuqǐ	CE	I'm sorry.
26. 給	gěi	V	to give
27. 水	shuǐ	N	water

Dialogue: *Pinyin*

Xiǎo Gāo: Shéi ya?

Wáng Péng: Shì wǒ, Wáng Péng, hái yǒu Lǐ Yǒu.

Xiǎo Gāo: Qǐng jìn, qǐng jìn! Lǐ Yǒu, kuài jìnlai! Lái, wǒ jièshào yí xià [G1], zhè

                    shì wǒ jiějie, Gāo Xiǎoyīn.

Lǐ Yǒu: Xiǎoyīn, nǐ hǎo. Rènshi nǐ hěn gāoxìng [1].

Gāo Xiǎoyīn: Rènshi nǐmen wǒ yě hěn gāoxìng.

Lǐ Yǒu: Nǐmen jiā hěn dà [G2], yě hěn piàoliang.

Xiǎo Gāo: Shì ma? [2]. Qǐng zuò, qǐng zuò.

Wáng Péng: Xiǎoyīn, nǐ zài [G3] nǎr gōngzuò?

Gāo Xiǎoyīn: Wǒ zài xuéxiào gōngzuò. Nǐmen xiǎng hē diǎnr [G1] shénme?

                    Yǒu chá, kāfēi, hái yǒu píjiǔ.

Wáng Péng: Wǒ hē píjiǔ ba [G4].

Lǐ Yǒu: Wǒ bù hē jiǔ. Wǒ yào yì bēi kělè, kěyǐ ma?

Gāo xiǎoyīn: Duìbuqǐ, wǒmen méiyǒu kělè.

Lǐ Yǒu: Nà gěi wǒ yì bēi shuǐ ba.

How many of the five drinks in the picture can you name in Chinese?

Dialogue: *Chinese*

小　高：誰呀？

王　朋：是我，王朋，還有李友。

小　高：請進，請進！李友，快進來！來，我介紹一下^(G1)，這是我姐姐，高小音。

李　友：小音，你好。認識你很高興⁽¹⁾。

高小音：認識你們我也很高興。

李　友：你們家很大^(G2)，也很漂亮。

小　高：是嗎？⁽²⁾。請坐，請坐。

王　朋：小音，你在^(G3)哪兒工作？

高小音：我在學校工作。你們想喝點兒^(G1)什麼？有茶、咖啡，還有啤酒。

王　朋：我喝啤酒吧^(G4)。

李　友：我不喝酒。我要一杯可樂，可以嗎？

高小音：對不起，我們沒有可樂。

李　友：那給我一杯水吧。

Notes:

(1) 認識你很高興 (Rènshi nǐ hěn gāoxìng) is the Chinese translation of "I'm glad to be acquainted," and may therefore sound rather western to some Chinese speakers. However, the traditional Chinese equivalent polite formulae have now generally become obsolete. For this reason such expressions as 認識你很高興 (Rènshi nǐ hěn gāoxìng) and 你好 (Nǐ hǎo) are gradually gaining acceptance among the Chinese.

(2) 是嗎 is not a question here, although it takes a question mark. It is an expression commonly used in showing modesty when receiving a compliment. Another phrase which can be used for the same purpose is 哪裏(nǎli). The original meaning of 哪裏 is

"where?" When paid a compliment, some Chinese people would say, "哪裏 (nǎli)" or "哪裏，哪裏 (nǎli, nǎli)." In recent times, however, 哪裏 has become somewhat old fashioned.

NARRATIVE: *At Friend's House*

Vocabulary

1.	玩(兒)	wán(r)	V	to have fun; to play
2.	圖書館	túshūguǎn	N	library
3.	瓶	píng	M	bottle
4.	一起	yìqǐ	Adv	together
5.	聊天(兒)	liáo tiān(r)	VO	to chat
6.	才	cái	Adv	not until (indicating that the time is late or has been long)
7.	回家	huí jiā	VO	to go home
	回	huí	V	to return

Narrative: *Pinyin*

Zuótiān wǎnshang, Wáng Péng hé Lǐ Yǒu qù Xiǎo Gāo jiā wánr. Zài Xiǎo Gāo jiā, tāmen rènshile (G5) Xiǎo Gāo de jiějie. Tā jiào Gāo Xiǎoyīn, zài xuéxiào de túshūguǎn gōngzuò. Xiǎo Gāo qǐng Wáng Péng hē píjiǔ, Wáng Péng hēle liǎng píng. Lǐ Yǒu bù hējiǔ, zhǐ hē le yì bēi shuǐ. Tāmen yìqǐ liáotiānr, kàn diànshì. Wáng Péng hé Lǐ Yǒu wǎnshang shí'èr diǎn cái (G6) huíjiā.

Narrative: *Chinese*

昨天晚上，王朋和李友去小高家玩兒。在小高家，他們認識了^(G5)小高的姐姐。她叫高小音，在學校的圖書館工作。小高請王朋喝啤酒，王朋喝了兩瓶。李友不喝酒，只喝了一杯水。他們一起聊天兒、看電視。王朋和李友晚上十二點才^(G6)回家。

Supplementary Vocabulary

1.	打工	dǎgōng	VO	to have a part-time job
2.	好吃	hǎochī	Adj	good to eat; delicious
3.	好喝	hǎohē	Adj	good to drink; tasty
4.	好看	hǎokàn	Adj	good-looking
5.	好玩(兒)	hǎowán(r)	Adj	fun
6.	可口可樂	kěkǒukělè	N	Coke
7.	百事可樂	bǎishìkělè	N	Pepsi
8.	雪碧	xuěbì	N	Sprite
9.	汽水(兒)	qìshuǐ(r)	N	soft drink; soda pop
10.	礦泉水	kuàngquánshuǐ	N	mineral water

Can you say the Chinese name of the drink on the left side?

GRAMMAR

1. <u>一下</u> (yí xià{r}) and (一)<u>點兒</u> ({yì} diǎnr) Moderating the Tone of Voice

Following a verb, both 一下 (yí xià{r}) and (一) 點兒 ({yì} diǎnr) can make the tone of voice moderate and more polite. When used in this sense, 一下 quantifies the verb which may or may not take an object, while (一) 點兒 quantifies the object of the verb.

(1) 你看一下，這是誰的照片？

Nǐ kàn yí xià, zhè shì shéi de zhàopiàn?

(Have a look. Whose photo is this?)

(2) 你想吃點兒什麼？

Nǐ xiǎng chī diǎnr shénme?

(What would you like to eat?)

(3) 你進來一下。

Nǐ jìnlai yí xià.

(Come in for a minute.)

(4) 你 喝一點兒啤酒吧。

Nǐ hē yīdiǎnr píjiǔ ba.

(Have some beer.)

2. Adjectives Used as Predicates

In Chinese an adjective can be used as a predicate without being preceded by the verb 是 (shì, to be).

(1) 我今天很高興。

Wǒ jīntiān hěn gāoxìng.

(I'm very happy today.)

(2) 他妹妹很漂亮。

Tā mèimei hěn piàoliang.

(His younger sister is very pretty.)

(3) 那個電影很好。

    Nàge diànyǐng hěn hǎo.

    (That movie is very good.)

(4) 你們學校很大。

    Nǐmen xuéxiào hěn dà.

    (Your school is very large.)

Note: When an adjective is used as a predicate, it is usually modified by a modifier like 很 (hěn, very). 很 (hěn) is not as strong as its English counterpart "very." In certain contexts Chinese adjectives can be inherently comparative. If that is the case, 很 (hěn) is not to be used before the adjective.

(5) A: 姐姐漂亮還是妹妹漂亮？

    Jiějie piàoliang háishi mèimei piàoliang?

    (Who is prettier, the older sister or the younger sister?)

    B: 妹妹漂亮。

    Mèimei piàoliang.

    (The younger sister is prettier).

3. 在 (zài, at; in; on)

    The preposition 在 (zài) plus a noun can indicate a location. When the phrase is placed before a verb, it indicates the location of the action.
For example:

(1) 你在哪兒工作？

    Nǐ zài nǎr gōngzuò?

    (Where do you work?)

(2) 我在這個學校學中文。

    Wǒ zài zhège xuéxiào xué Zhōngwén.

    (I study Chinese at this school.)

(3) 我不喜歡在家看電影。

    Wǒ bù xǐhuan zài jiā kàn diànyǐng.

    (I don't like watching movies at home.)

4. The Particle of Mood 吧 (ba)

吧 (ba) is often used at the end of an imperative or suggestive sentence, making the tone of speech much softer.
For example:

(1) 你喝啤酒吧。

   Nǐ hē píjiǔ ba.

   (Have some beer.)

(2) 請進來吧。

   Qǐng jǐnlai ba.

   (Come in, please.)

5. The Particle 了 (le) (I)

The dynamic particle 了 (le) signifies realization or completion of an action or an event. The completion of the action or an event can take place in the future as in (4) below. Therefore it is not the equivalent of the past tense in English. 了 (le) can be used after a verb or at the end of a sentence.

(1) 媽媽喝了一杯水。

   Māma hēle yì bēi shuǐ.

   (Mom had a glass of water.)

(2) 昨天晚上我去小高家玩兒了。

   Zuótiān wǎnshang wǒ qù Xiǎo Gāo jiā wánr le.

   (Yesterday evening I went to Little Gao's home for a visit.)

(3) 星期一小高請我喝了一瓶啤酒。

   Xīngqīyī Xiǎo Gāo qǐng wǒ hēle yì píng píjiǔ.

   (Monday Little Gao bought a beer for me.)

(4) 明天我吃了晚飯去看電影。

   Míngtiān wǒ chīle wǎnfàn qù kàn diànyǐng.

   (Tomorrow I'll go see a movie after I have dinner.)

Note: There is often a specific time phrase in a sentence with the dynamic particle 了 (le) such as 昨天晚上 (zuótiān wǎnshang, last night) in (2), 星期一 (xīngqīyī, Monday) in (3), 明天 (míngtiān, tomorrow) in (4). When 了 (le) is used between the verb and the object which is not followed by any other verb phrases or clauses, the object must be preceded by a modifier. The most common modifier for the object is a numeral-measure word combination, e.g. ,

一杯 (yì bēi, one cup, one glass) in sentence (1),

一瓶 (yì píng, one bottle) in sentence (3).

If there are other phrases or sentences following the object, the object does not have to have a modifier, as in Sentence (4).

To say that an action did not take place in the past, use 没(有)(méi {yǒu}). Do not use 不...了 (bù...le) or 没有...了.

For example:

(5) 昨天我沒有聽音樂。

Zuótiān wǒ méiyǒu tīng yīnyuè.

(I didn't listen to the music yesterday.)

(5a) **Incorrect:** 昨天我不聽音樂了。

Zuótiān wǒ bù tīng yīnyuè le.

(5b) **Incorrect:** 昨天我沒有聽音樂了。

Zuótiān wǒ méiyǒu tīng yīnyuè le.

Interrogative forms:

(6) A: 你吃了嗎?

Nǐ chīle ma?

(Did you eat?)

B: 我沒吃。

Wǒ méi chī.

(No, I did not.)

(7) 你吃飯了沒有?

Nǐ chīfànle méiyǒu?

(Have you eaten?)

(8) A: 你喝了幾杯水？

    Nǐ hēle jǐ bēi shuǐ?

    (How many glasses of water did you drink?)

    B: 我喝了一杯水。

    Wǒ hēle yì bēi shuǐ.

    (I drank one glass of water.)

A note on the phrase 認識了 (rènshi le)：認識 (rènshi, to know) is a verb which usually indicates not an action but a state, and that is why it is usually not followed by 了. However, it can sometimes denote the start of the state, meaning "to get to know" or "to become acquainted with." When 認識 is used in the latter sense, the 了 that follows indicates the completion of the transition from not knowing to knowing. Compare:

(9) 我認識高小音。

    Wǒ rènshi Gāo Xiǎoyīn.

    (I know Gao Xiaoyin.)

(10) 我昨天認識了高小音。

    Wǒ zuótiān rènshi le Gāo Xiǎoyīn.

    (I got acquainted with Gao Xiaoyin yesterday.)

6. The Adverb 才 (cái)

才 (cái) can indicate that an action happened later than expected.

(1) 我六點請他吃晚飯，他六點半才來。

    Wǒ liù diǎn qǐng tā chī wǎnfàn, tā liù diǎn bàn cái lái.

    (I was going to treat him to dinner at six. He didn't come till six-thirty.)

(2) 我昨天十二點才回家。

    Wǒ zuótiān shí'èr diǎn cái huíjiā.

    (I didn't go home yesterday till twelve o'clock.)

(3) 她晚上很晚才睡覺。

    Tā wǎnshang hěn wǎn cái shuì jiào.

    (She goes to bed very late in the evening.)

PATTERN DRILLS

A.   <u>一下</u> (yí xià)

1.	Wǒ kàn	<u>yí xià</u>.	
2.	Nǐ jièshào		
3.	Nǐ zuò		
4.	Wǒ tīng		
5.	Nǐ qù		
6.	Nǐ lái		

1.   我看   <u>一下</u>。

2.   你介紹

3.   你坐

4.   我聽

5.   你去

6.   你來

B. Adjectives Used as Predicates

1.	<u>Xiǎo Gāo de</u>	jiā	<u>hěn</u>	piàoliang.
2.		xuéxiào		dà.
3.		yīshēng		máng.
4.		shū		yǒu yìsi.
5.		jiějie		gāoxìng.
6.		dìdi		gāo.
7.		lǎoshī		hǎo.
8.		tóngxué		hǎo.

1. <u>小高的</u>   家   <u>很</u>   漂亮。

2.   學校   大。

3.   醫生   忙。

4.   書   有意思。

5.   姐姐   高興。

6. <u>小高的</u>　　弟弟　　<u>很</u>　　高。

7. 　　　　　老師　　　　　好。

8. 　　　　　同學　　　　　好。

C. <u>在</u> (zài)

C1

1. <u>Wáng Péng he Lǐ Yǒu</u>　<u>zài</u>　túshūguǎn　　kàn shū.
2. 　　　　　　　　　　　　　jiā　　　　　tīng yīnyuè.
3. 　　　　　　　　　　　　　túshūguǎn　　gōngzuò.
4. 　　　　　　　　　　　　　jiā　　　　　kàn diànshì.
5. 　　　　　　　　　　　　　Xiǎo Gāo jiā　　hē kāfēi.
6. 　　　　　　　　　　　　　Wáng lǎoshī jiā　liáo tiān.
7. 　　　　　　　　　　　　　Xiǎo Bái jiā　　chī fàn.
8. 　　　　　　　　　　　　　xuéxiào　　　dǎ qiú.

1. <u>王朋和李友</u>　　<u>在</u>　　圖書館　　看書。

2. 　　　　　　　　　　　　家　　　　聽音樂。

3. 　　　　　　　　　　　　圖書館　　工作。

4. 　　　　　　　　　　　　家　　　　看電視。

5. 　　　　　　　　　　　　小高家　　喝咖啡。

6. 　　　　　　　　　　　　王老師家　聊天。

7. 　　　　　　　　　　　　小白家　　吃飯。

8. 　　　　　　　　　　　　學校　　　打球。

C2 (Answer questions with 在.)

Example: Xiǎo Gāo zài nǎr gōngzuò? (xuéxiào)
　　　　---> Xiǎo Gāo zài xuéxiào gōngzuò.

小高在<u>哪兒</u>工作？（學校）

-->小高在<u>學校</u>工作。

1. Zhāng yīshēng zài nǎr tīng yīnyuè?　　(jiā)
2. Xiǎo Wáng zài nǎr dǎ qiú?　　(xuéxiào)
3. Xiǎo Gāo de mèimei zài nǎr kàn shū?　　(túshūguǎn)
4. Xiǎo Lǐ hé Xiǎo Bái zài nǎr kàn diānyǐng?　　(xuéxiào)
5. Wáng Péng hé Lǐ Yǒu zài nǎr liáo tiānr?　　(Xiǎo Gāo jiā)
6. Xiǎo Gāo de jiějie zài nǎr gōngzuò?　　(túshūguǎn)
7. Xiǎo Zhāng zài nǎr shuìjiào?　　(jiā)

1. 張醫生在哪兒聽音樂？　　（家）

2. 小王在哪兒打球？　　（學校）

3. 小高的妹妹在哪兒看書？　　（圖書館）

4. 小李和小白在哪兒看電影？　　（學校）

5. 王朋和李友在哪兒聊天兒？　　（小高家）

6. 小高的姐姐在哪兒工作？　　（圖書館）

7. 小張在哪兒睡覺？　　（家）

D. **點兒** (diǎnr)

1. Nǐ	xiǎng	chī	diǎnr	shénme?
2. Xiǎo Bái		tīng		
3. Nǐ		zuò		
4. Zhāng lǜshī		chī		
5. Lǐ yīshēng, nín		hē		

1. 你　　　　想　　吃　　點兒　什麼？

2. 小白　　　　　　聽

3. 你　　　　　　　做

4. 張律師　　　　　吃

5. 李醫生，您　　　喝

E. 了 (le)

1.Tā zuótiān wǎnshang	hē	**le**	sì bēi	shuǐ.
2.	kàn		liǎng ge	diànyǐng.
3.	hē		wǔ bēi	kělè.
4.	hē		liǎng píng	píjiǔ.
5.	hē		liù bēi	chá.
6.	chàng		sān ge	gē.
7.	tiào		yí ge	wǔ.

1. 他昨天晚上	喝	了	四杯	水。
2.	看		兩個	電影。
3.	喝		五杯	可樂。
4.	喝		兩瓶	啤酒。
5.	喝		六杯	茶。
6.	唱		三個	歌。
7.	跳		一個	舞。

F. 才 (cái)

1. Wǒmen	liù diǎn	chī fàn,	tā	liù diǎn bàn	cái lái.
2.	jiǔ diǎn	tiào wǔ,		shí diǎn	
3.	qī diǎn	kàn diànyǐng,		bā diǎn	
4.	bā diǎn bàn	hē kāfēi,		jiǔ diǎn	
5.	qī diǎn	chī wǎnfàn,		qī diǎn bàn	
6.	jiǔ diǎn shí fēn	dǎ qiú,		jiǔ diǎn bàn	
7.	bā diǎn	tīng yīnyuè,		bā diǎn bàn	
8.	liù diǎn shíwǔ fēn	gōngzuò,		liù diǎn bàn	
9.	wǔ diǎn	qù zhǎo Gāo lǎoshī,		liù diǎn èrshí fēn	

1. 我們	六點	吃飯，	他	六點半	才來。
2.	九點	跳舞，		十點	

3. <u>我們</u>   七點   看電影，   <u>他</u>   八點   <u>才來</u>。

4.   八點半   喝咖啡，   九點

5.   七點   吃晚飯，   七點半

6.   九點十分   打球，   九點半

7.   八點   聽音樂，   八點半

8.   六點十五分   工作，   六點半

9.   五點   去找高老師，   六點二十分

Can you make a story out of the four pictures above?

Don't forget to mention the time in each picture!

ENGLISH TEXT

Dialogue

Little Gao:	Who is it?
Wang Peng:	It's me, Wang Peng. Li You is here, too.
Little Gao:	Please come in. Please come in, Li You. Let me introduce you to one another. This is my sister, Gao Xiaoyin.
Li You.	How do you do, Xiaoyin! Pleased to meet you.
Gao Xiaoyin:	Pleased to meet you, too.
Li You:	Your home is very big, and very beautiful, too.
Little Gao.	Really? Sit down, please.
Wang Peng:	Xiaoyin, where do you work?
Gao Xiaoyin:	I work at a school. What would you like to drink? We have tea, coffee, and beer.
Wang Peng:	I'll have a beer.
Li You:	I don't drink. I'd like to have a glass of coke, can I?
Miss Gao:	I'm sorry. We don't have coke.
Li You:	Then please give me a glass of water.

Do you know the name of the girl standing next to Little Gao?

Narrative

Last night Wang Peng and Li You went to Little Gao's home for a visit. At Little Gao's home they met Little Gao's older sister. Her name was Gao Xiaoyin. She worked at a school library. Little Gao offered beer to Wang Peng. Wang Peng had two bottles of beer. Li You did not drink. She just had a glass of water. They talked and watched TV together. Wang Peng and Li You did not get home until twelve o'clock.

Use what you have learned so far to describe the picture above.
You may also write a dialogue for them.

Lesson Six   Making Appointments
第六課　　　　約時間

DIALOGUE I: *CALLING ONE'S TEACHER*

Vocabulary

1. 給	gěi	Prep	to; for
2. 打電話	dǎ diànhuà	VO	to make a phone call
電話	diànhuà	N	telephone
話	huà	N	speech; talk; words
3. 喂	wèi	Interj	Hello!; Hey!
4. 在	zài	V	to be present; to be at (a place)
5. 就	jiù	Adv	(indicating verification of someone mentioned before)

6.	哪	nǎ/něi	QPr	which
7.	位	wèi	M	(a polite measure word for people)
8.	下午	xiàwǔ	T	afternoon
9.	時間	shíjiān	T	time
10.	幾	jǐ	Nu	some; a few (stands for an indefinite number less than ten)
11.	問題	wèntí	N	question; problem
12.	要	yào	AV	will; be going to
13.	開會	kāi huì	VO	to have a meeting
	開	kāi	V	to hold (a meeting, party, etc.)
14.	上午	shàngwǔ	T	morning
15.	節	jié	M	(a measure word for class period)
16.	課	kè	N	class; lesson
17.	年級	niánjí	N	grade in school
18.	考試	kǎoshì	V/N	to give or take a test; test
	考	kǎo	V	to give or take a test
19.	以後	yǐhòu	T	after
20.	有空(兒)	yǒu kòng(r)	VO	to have time
21.	要是	yàoshi	Conj	if
22.	方便	fāngbiàn	Adj	convenient
23.	到…去	dào…qù		to go to (a place)

24	辦公室	bàngōngshì	N	office
25	行	xíng	Adj	all right; O.K.
26	沒問題	méi wèntí	CE	no problem
27	等	děng	V	to wait; to wait for
28	不客氣	bú kèqi	CE	You are welcome. Don't be (so) polite.
	客氣	kèqi	Adj	polite

Dialogue I: *Pinyin*

(Lǐ Yǒu gěi [G1] lǎoshī dǎ diànhuà)

Lǐ Yǒu: Wéi, qǐng wèn, Wáng lǎoshī zài ma?

Wáng lǎoshī: Wǒ jiù shì. Nín shì nǎ wèi?

Lǐ Yǒu: Lǎoshī, nín hǎo. Wǒ shì Lǐ Yǒu.

Wáng lǎoshī: Lǐ Yǒu, nǐ hǎo, yǒu shì ma?

Lǐ Yǒu: Lǎoshī, jīntiān xiàwǔ nín yǒu shíjiān ma? Wǒ xiǎng wèn nín jǐ ge wèntí.

Wáng lǎoshī: Duìbuqǐ, jīntiān xiàwǔ wǒ yào [G2] kāi huì.

Lǐ Yǒu: Míngtiān ne?

Wáng lǎoshī: Míngtiān shàngwǔ wǒ yǒu liǎng jié [1] kè, xiàwǔ sāndiǎn zhōng yào gěi èr niánjí kǎoshì.

Lǐ Yǒu: Nín shénme shíhòu yǒukòng?

Wáng lǎoshī: Míngtiān sì diǎn yǐhòu cái yǒu kòng.

Lǐ Yǒu: Yàoshì nín fāngbiàn, sìdiǎn bàn wǒ dào nín de bàngōngshì qù, xíng ma?

Wáng lǎoshī: Sì diǎn bàn, méi wèntí. Wǒ zài bàngōngshì děng nǐ.

Lǐ Yǒu: Xièxie nín.

Wáng lǎoshī: Bú kèqi.

Dialogue I: *Chinese*

（李友給^(G1)老師打電話）

李　　友：喂，請問王老師在嗎？

王老師：我就是。您是哪位？

李　　友：老師，您好。我是李友。

王老師：李友，你好，有事嗎？

李　　友：老師，今天下午您有時間嗎？我想問您
　　　　　幾個問題。

王老師：對不起，今天下午我要^(G2)開會。

李　　友：明天呢？

王老師：明天上午我有兩節⁽¹⁾課，下午三點鐘要
　　　　　給二年級考試。

李　　友：您什麼時候有空？

王老師：明天四點以後才有空。

李　　友：要是您方便，四點半我到您的辦公室
　　　　　去，行嗎？

王老師：四點半，沒問題。我在辦公室等你。

李　　友：謝謝您。

王老師：不客氣。

Notes:

(1) The character 節 (jié), which literally means "segment," is here a measure word for class periods. It should not be used **as a measure** word for courses, for which the measure word 門 (mén) is used instead. **Compare** 三節課 (sān jié kè, three classes) with 三門課 (sān mén kè, three courses).

DIALOGUE II: *CALLING A FRIEND FOR HELP*

Vocabulary

1. 幫忙	bāng máng	VO	to help; to do someone a favor
2. 別客氣	bié kèqi	CE	Don't be so polite!
別	bié		don't (See G3)
3. 下個星期	xiàge xīngqī	T	next week
下	xià		next (used before a noun or measure word to indicate coming later in time order)
4. 中文	Zhōngwén	N	Chinese language
文	wén		language; script; written language
5. 幫	bāng	V	to help
6. 練習	liànxí	V	to practice
7. 説	shuō	V	to say; to speak
8. 啊	a	P	(used at the end of a sentence to emphasize agreement, exclamation, interrogation, etc.)
9. 但是	dànshì	Conj	but
10. 得	děi	AV	must; have to
11. 知道	zhīdao	V	to know (See Textual Note 2 for Dialogue II)
12. 回來	huí lai	VC	to come back

Dialogue II: *Pinyin*

Lǐ Yǒu:	Wèi, qǐng wèn Wáng Péng zài ma?
Wáng Péng:	Wǒ jiù shì. Nǐ shì Lǐ Yǒu ba? Yǒu shì ma?
Lǐ Yǒu:	Wǒ xiǎng qǐng nǐ bāngmáng.
Wáng Péng:	Bié (G3) kèqì, yǒu shénme shì?
Lǐ Yǒu:	Wǒ xiàge xīngqī yào kǎo Zhōngwén, nǐ bāng wǒ liànxí shuō Zhōngwén, hǎo ma?
Wáng Péng:	Hǎo a, dànshì nǐ děi (G4) qǐng wǒ hē kāfēi.
Lǐ Yǒu:	Hē kāfēi, méi wèntí. Jīntiān wǎnshang nǐ yǒu kòngr ma?
Wáng Péng:	Jīntiān wǎnshang yǒu rén qǐng wǒ chīfàn, bù zhīdao shénme shíhou huílai (G5). Wǒ huílai yǐhòu gěi nǐ dǎ diànhuà ba.
Lǐ Yǒu:	Hǎo ba, wǒ děng nǐ de diànhuà.

Dialogue II: *Chinese*

李友：喂，請問王朋在嗎？

王朋：我就是。你是李友吧？有事嗎？

李友：我想請你幫忙。

王朋：別(G3)客氣，有什麼事？

李友：我下個星期要考中文(1)，你幫我練習說中
文，好嗎？

王朋：好啊，但是你得(G4)請我喝咖啡。

李友：喝咖啡，沒問題。今天晚上你有空兒嗎？

王朋：今天晚上有人請我吃飯，不知道(2)什麼時
候回來(G5)。我回來以後給你打電話吧。

李友：好吧，我等你的電話。

Notes:

(1) 漢語 (Hànyǔ) and 中文 (Zhōngwén) both refer to the Chinese language. 漢語 can imply a stress on the colloquial aspect of the language while 中文 can be more emphatic on the written form, but in most cases the two terms are used interchangeably.

(2) 知道 (zhīdao) should not be taken as entirely synonymous to 認識 (rènshi), although both words can be translated into English as "to know." 知道 (zhīdao) typically takes an object that stands for something or some event, while the object of 認識 (rènshi) is usually a person or a written character. The object of 知道 (zhīdao) can sometimes be a person or a written character as well, but the meaning is different. The sentence "我知道他"(Wǒ zhīdao tā) suggests a knowledge about that person: "I heard about him." It does not indicate a personal acquaintance as does the word 認識 (rènshi).

Supplementary Vocabulary

1.	中午	zhōngwǔ	T	noon
2.	法文	Fǎwén	N	the French language
3.	日文	Rìwén	N	the Japanese language
4.	德文	Déwén	N	the German language
5.	韓國	Hánguó	N	Korea
6.	韓文	Hánwén	N	the Korean language
7.	俄國	Éguó	N	Russia
8.	俄文	Éwén	N	the Russian language
9.	西班牙	Xībānyá	N	Spain
10.	西班牙文	Xībānyáwén	N	the Spanish language
11.	意大利	Yìdàlì	N	Italy
12.	意大利文	Yìdàlìwén	N	the Italian language
13.	葡萄牙	Pútáoyá	N	Portugal
14.	葡萄牙文	Pútáoyáwén	N	the Portuguese language
15.	希臘	Xīlà	N	Greece
16.	希臘文	Xīlàwén	N	the Greek language
17.	拉丁文	Lādīngwén	N	Latin
18.	越南	Yuènán	N	Vietnam
19.	菲律賓	Fēilǜbīn	N	the Philippines
20.	泰國	Tàiguó	N	Thailand
21.	馬來西亞	Mǎláixīyà	N	Malaysia
22.	夏威夷	Xiàwēiyí	N	Hawaii

GRAMMAR

1. The Preposition 給 (gěi)

給 (gěi) is both a verb and a preposition. In Chinese a preposition is generally combined with a noun or a pronoun following it to form a prepositional phrase. It appears before verbs as an adverbial.

For example:

(1) 他給我打了一個電話。

   Tā gěi wǒ dǎle yí gè diànhuà.

   (He gave me a call.)

(2) 他是誰？請你給我們介紹一下。

   Tā shì shéi? Qǐng nǐ gěi wǒmen jièshào yí xià.

   (Who is he? Please introduce him to us.)

(3) 你有你姐姐的照片嗎？給我看一下，行嗎？

   Nǐ yǒu nǐ jiějie de zhàopiàn ma? Gěi wǒ kàn yí xià, xíng ma?

   (Do you have a picture of your sister? Can you let me have a look?)

2. The Auxiliary Verb 要 (yào, will; be going to) (I)

The modal verb 要 (yào) has several meanings. In this lesson, 要 (yào) indicates a future action.

Examples:

(1) 明天我要去小白家玩。

   Míngtiān wǒ yào qù Xiǎo Bái jiā wán.

   (Tomorrow I'm going to visit Little Bai.)

(2) 今天晚上妹妹要去看電影。

   Jīntiān wǎnshang mèimei yào qù kàn diànyǐng.

   (This evening my younger sister is going to see a movie.)

(3) 下午我們要開會。

   Xiàwǔ wǒmen yào kāihuì.

   (This afternoon we are going to have a meeting.)

3. **别** (bié, don't)

别 (bié, don't) can be used to admonish someone to refrain from doing something.

(1) 你別說！

Nǐ bié shuō!

(Don't tell.)

(2) 別進來！

Bié jìnlai!

(Don't come in.)

(3) 那個電影沒有意思，你別看。

Nàge diànyǐng méiyǒu yìsi, nǐ bié kàn.

(That movie is boring. Don't go to see it.)

4. The Auxiliary Verb 得 (děi, must)

The modal verb 得 (děi) means "need" or "must".

(1) 老師三點鐘給你打了一個電話，你得給老師打個

電話。

Lǎoshī sān diǎnzhōng gěi nǐ dǎle yí ge diànhuà, nǐ děi gěi lǎoshī dǎ
ge diànhuà.

(The teacher called you at 3 o'clock. You'd better give him a call.)

(2) 我有事，得去學校。

Wǒ yǒu shì, děi qù xuéxiào.

(I've some business [to attend to]. I must go to the school.)

Note: The negative form for 得 (děi, must) is 不用 (bú yòng, need not; not have to) or
不必 (need not; not have to), but not 不得. Therefore, the correct way to say "You
don't have to go to the school." in Chinese is A and not B below.

Correct: "你不用去學校。" (Nǐ bú yòng qù xuéxiào.)

Incorrect: "你不得去學校。" (Nǐ bù děi qù xuéxiào.)

5. Directional Complements (I)

來/去 (lái/qù, to come/go) can serve as a directional complement after such verbs as 進 (jìn, to enter) and 回 (huí, to return). 來 (lái, to come) signifies movement toward the speaker. 去 (qù, to go) signifies movement away from the speaker.

(1) [**A** is at home on the phone.]

A: 你什麼時候回來？

Nǐ shénme shíhou huílai?

(When are you coming home?)

B: 我六點回去。

Wǒ liù diàn huíqu.

(I'm going back home at six.)

(2) [**A** is outside, and **B** is inside. **A** knocks on the door.]

B: 進來！   Jìnlai!   (Come in.)

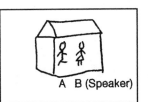 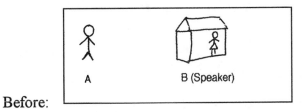

Before: After:

(3) [Both **A** and **B** are outside. **A** tells **B** to go inside.]

A: 進去！   Jìnqu!   (Go in.)

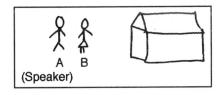 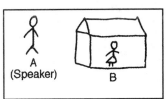

Before: After:

PATTERN DRILLS

A. 給 (gěi) as preposition

1. Wǒ	gěi nǐ	jièshào yí xià.
2. Lǐ lǎoshī		kàn tā de shū.
3. Xiǎo Gāo		kàn tā bàba māma de zhàopiān.
4. Xiǎo Wáng		tīng Zhōngguó yīnyuè.
5. Tā		jièshào yí ge péngyou.
6. Gāo Xiǎoyīn		hē Zhōngguó píjiǔ.

1. 我　　　　　給你　　　　介紹一下。

2. 李老師　　　　　　　　看她的書。

3. 小高　　　　　　　　　看他爸爸媽媽的照片。

4. 小王　　　　　　　　　聽中國音樂。

5. 她　　　　　　　　　　介紹一個朋友。

6. 高小音　　　　　　　　喝中國啤酒。

B. 要 (yào) indicating a future action

1. Míngtiān	wǒ yào	qù tiào wǔ.
2. Zhège zhōumò		qù zhǎo Gāo Xiǎoyīn.
3. Jīntiān wǎnshang		qǐng Wáng Péng hē kāfēi.
4. Míngtiān xiàwǔ		qù Lǐ lǎoshī de bàngōngshì.
5. Jīntiān xiàwǔ		wèn Xiǎo Bái yí ge wèntí.
6. Míngtiān wǎnshang		qù Xiǎo Zhāng de xuéxiào kàn diànyǐng.
7. Míngtiān shàngwǔ		qù Xiǎo Gāo jiā liànxí Zhōngwén.
8. Zhège zhōumò		gěi Wáng lǎoshī dǎ diànhuà.
9. Zhège zhōumò		gěi Xiǎo Gāo jièshào yí ge péngyou.

1. 明天　　　　　我要　　　　去跳舞。

2. 這個週末　　　　　　　　去找高小音。

3. 今天晚上　　　　　　　　請王朋喝咖啡。

4. 明天下午　　　　　<u>我要</u>　　　去李老師的辦公室。

5. 今天下午　　　　　　　　　　問小白一個問題。

6. 明天晚上　　　　　　　　　　去小張的學校看電影。

7. 明天上午　　　　　　　　　　去小高家練習中文。

8. 這個週末　　　　　　　　　　給王老師打電話。

9. 這個週末　　　　　　　　　　給小高介紹一個朋友。

C. <u>要是</u> (yàoshi, if)

1. Yàoshi	nǐ jīntiān méiyǒu kòngr, míngtiān	zěnmeyàng?
2.	nǐ bù xiǎng kàn diànshì, wǒmen tīng yīnyuè,	
3.	nǐ juéde dǎ qiú méiyǒu yìsi, wǒmen qù kàn diànyǐng,	
4.	nǐ bù xǐhuan tiào wǔ, wǒmen liáo tiānr,	
5.	jīntiān bù fāngbiàn, míngtiān,	
6.	bù xǐhuan hēchá, wǒmen hē píjiǔ,	
7.	nǐ jīntiān qǐng wǒ hē kāfēi, wǒ míngtiān qǐng nǐ kàn diànyǐng,	
8.	nǐ xiǎng wèn wǒ wèntí, xiàwǔ lái wǒde bàngōngshì,	

1. <u>要是</u>　你今天沒有空兒，明天　　　　　　　<u>怎麼樣</u>？

2.　　　　你不想看電視，我們聽音樂，

3.　　　　你覺得打球沒有意思，我們去看電影，

4.　　　　你不喜歡跳舞，我們聊天兒，

5.　　　　今天不方便，明天

6.　　　　不喜歡喝茶，我們喝啤酒，

7.　　　　你今天請我喝咖啡，我明天請你看電影，

8.　　　　你想問我問題，下午來我的辦公室，

D. 別 (bié, don't)

1. <u>Nǐ bié</u>	dǎ qiú,	<u>nǐ děi</u>	kàn shū.
2.	hē chá,		shuì jiào.
3.	kàn diànshì,		gěi Wáng lǎoshī dǎ diànhuà.
4.	shuì jiào,		kàn shū.
5.	liáo tiānr,		qù kāihuì.
6.	hē píjiǔ,		kǎoshì.
7.	chī fàn,		dǎ qiú.
8.	qù Xiǎo Gāo jiā,		zài jiā děng nǐ bàba māma de diànhuà.
9.	liáo tiānr,		liànxí Zhōngwén.

1.	<u>你別</u>	打球，	<u>你得</u> 看書。
2.		喝茶，	睡覺。
3.		看電視，	給王老師打電話。
4.		睡覺，	看書。
5.		聊天，	去開會。
6.		喝啤酒，	考試。
7.		吃飯，	打球。
8.		去小高家，	在家等你爸爸媽媽的電話。
9.		聊天兒，	練習中文。

E. 得 (děi, have to, must)

1. Jīntiān	<u>wǒ děi</u>	qù zhǎo Wáng lǎoshī.
2. Jīntiān wǎnshang		qù Xiǎo Gāo jiā liànxí Zhōngwén.
3. Zhège zhōumò		qù túshūguǎn kàn shū.
4. Jīntiān xiàwǔ		qù xuéxiào kāi huì.
5. Míngtiāng wǎnshang		qù Xiǎo Bái jiā chī wǎnfàn.
6. Míngtiān shàngwǔ		qù Wánglǎoshī de bàngōngshì.
7. Míngtiān xiàwǔ		hé Wáng Péng liànxí Zhōngwén.
8. Míngtiān wǎnshang		qù xuéxiào liànxí chànggē.
9. Jīntiān wǎnshang		zài jiā liànxí tiàowǔ.

1. 今天	我 得	去找王老師。
2. 今天晚上		去小高家練習中文。
3. 這個週末		去圖書館看書。
4. 今天下午		去學校開會。
5. 明天晚上		去小白家吃晚飯。
6. 明天上午		去王老師的辦公室。
7. 明天下午		和王朋練習中文。
8. 明天晚上		去學校練習唱歌。
9. 今天晚上		在家練習跳舞。

Write the numbers of the sentences above which are related to the pictures below.

( )

( )

( )

( )

( )

( )

ENGLISH TEXT

Dialogue I

(Li You is on the phone with her teacher.)

Li You: Hello, is Teacher Wang in?

Teacher Wang: This is he. Who is this, please?

Li You: Teacher, how are you. This is Li You.

Teacher Wang: Li You, how are you. What is going on?

Li You: Teacher, are you free this afternoon? I'd like to ask you a few questions.

Teacher Wang: I'm sorry. This afternoon I have to go to a meeting.

Li You: What about tomorrow?

Teacher Wang: Tomorrow morning I have two classes. Tomorrow afternoon at three o'clock I have to give an exam to the second-year class.

Li You: When you will be free?

Teacher Wang: I won't be free until after four o'clock tomorrow.

Li You: If it's convenient with you, I'll go to your office at four-thirty. Is that all right?

Teacher Wang: Four-thirty? No problem. I'll wait for you in my office.

Li You: Thank you.

Teacher Wang: You're welcome.

Dialogue II

(Li You and Wang Peng are talking on the phone.)

Li You: Hello, is Wang Peng there?

Wang Peng: This is he. Is this Li You? What's up?

Li You: I'd like to ask you for a favor.

Wang Peng: Don't be so polite. What is it?

Li You: Next week I have a Chinese exam. Could you help me practice speaking Chinese?

Wang Peng: Sure, but you must buy me a coffee.

Li You: Buy you a coffee? No problem. Are you free this evening?

Wang Peng: This evening someone is taking me to dinner. I don't know when I'll be back. Why don't I call you after I get back?

Li You. O.K. I'll wait for your call.

Lesson Seven   Studying Chinese
第七課   學中文

DIALOGUE I: *ASKING ABOUT AN EXAMINATION*

Vocabulary

1. 跟	gēn	Conj	and
2. 説話	shuō huà	VO	to talk
3. 上個星期	shàngge xīngqī	NP	last week
4. 得	de	P	(a particle used after a verb and before a descriptive complement)
5. 幫助	bāngzhù	V	to help
6. 復習	fùxí	V	to review

7. 字	zì	N	word; character
8. 寫	xiě	V	to write
9. 慢	màn	Adj	slow
10. 教	jiāo	V	to teach
11. 怎麼	zěnme	QPr	how; in what way (used to inquire about how to do things)
12. 就	jiù	Adv	(indicates that something takes place sooner than expected)
13. 學	xué	V	to study
14. 筆	bǐ	N	pen
15. 難	nán	Adj	difficult
16. 快	kuài	Adj	quick; fast
17. 哪裏	nǎli	CE	You flatter me (a polite reply to a compliment); not at all. Also see Note 2 for the Dialogue in L.5
18. 第	dì	prefix	(prefix for ordinal numbers)
19. 預習	yùxí	V	to preview
20. 語法	yǔfǎ	N	grammar
21. 容易	róngyì	Adj	easy
22. 多	duō	Adj	many; much
23. 懂	dǒng	V	to understand
24. 生詞	shēngcí	N	new words
25. 漢字	Hànzì	N	Chinese characters

26. 有一點兒 yǒu yìdiǎnr CE a little; somewhat
[Also see G5]

27. 不謝 bú xiè CE don't mention it; not at all

Dialogue I: *Pinyin*

(Wáng Péng gēn Lǐ Yǒu shuōhuà.)

Wáng Péng: Lǐ Yǒu, nǐ shàngge xīngqī kǎoshì kǎo de [G1] zěnmeyàng?

Lǐ Yǒu: Kǎo de búcuò, yīnwèi nǐ bāngzhù [1] wǒ fùxí, suǒyǐ kǎo de búcuò. Dànshì lǎoshī shuō wǒ Zhōngguózì xiě de tài [G2] màn!

Wáng Péng: Shì ma? Yǐhòu wǒ gēn nǐ yìqǐ liànxí xiě zì, jiāo nǐ zěnme xiě, hǎo bu hǎo?

Lǐ Yǒu: Nà tài hǎo le! Wǒmen xiànzài jiù [G3] xiě, gěi nǐ bǐ.

Wáng Péng: Hǎo, wǒ jiāo nǐ xiě "nán" zì.

Lǐ Yǒu: Nǐ xiě zì xiě de hěn hǎo, yě hěn kuài.

Wáng Péng: Nǎli, nǎli. Nǐ míngtiān yǒu Zhōngwén kè ma?

Lǐ Yǒu: Yǒu, míngtiān wǒmen xué dì-qī [G4] kè.

Wáng Péng: Nǐ yùxí le ma?

Lǐ Yǒu: Yùxí le. Dì-qī kè de yǔfǎ hěn róngyi, wǒ dōu dǒng, kěshì shēngcí tài duō, hànzì yě yǒu yìdiǎnr [G5] nán.

Wáng Péng: Jīntiān wǎnshang wǒ gēn nǐ yìqǐ liànxí ba.

Lǐ Yǒu: Hǎo, xièxie nǐ.

Wáng Péng: Bú xiè, wǎnshang jiàn.

What is the woman saying to the man?

You can find the answer in Dialogue I.

Dialogue I: *Chinese*

（王朋跟李友説話）

王朋：李友，你上個星期考試考得^(G1)怎麼樣？

李友：考得不錯，因爲你幫助⁽¹⁾我復習，所以考得
　　　不錯。但是老師説我中國字寫得太^(G2)慢！

王朋：是嗎？以後我跟你一起練習寫字，教你怎
　　　麼寫，好不好？

李友：那太好了！我們現在就^(G3)寫，給你筆。

王朋：好，我教你寫"難"字。

李友：你寫字寫得很好，也很快。

王朋：哪裏，哪裏。你明天有中文課嗎？

李友：有，明天我們學第七^(G4)課。

王朋：你預習了嗎？

李友：預習了。第七課的語法很容易，我都懂，
　　　可是生詞太多，漢字也有一點兒^(G5)難。

王朋：今天晚上我跟你一起練習吧。

李友：好，謝謝你。

王朋：不謝，晚上見。

(1) The verb 幫助, like 幫, takes an object, while the other verb 幫忙 does not.
Therefore, while we can say "他幫我練習中文" or "他幫助我練習中文," we should
never say "他幫忙我練習中文."

DIALOGUE II: *PREPARING FOR A CHINESE CLASS*

Vocabulary

1. 平常	píngcháng	T	usually
2. 早	zǎo	Adj	early
3. 怎麼	zěnme	QPr	how come (used to inquire about the cause of something, implying a degree of surprise or disapproval)
4. 這麼	zhème	Pr	so; such
5. 半夜	bànyè	T	midnight; small hours
6. 功課	gōngkè	N	schoolwork; homework
7. 朋友	péngyou	N	friend
8. 真(眞)**	zhēn	Adv	really
9. 大家	dàjiā	Pr	everybody
10. 早	zǎo		Good morning!
11. 開始	kāishǐ	V	to start
12. 上課	shàng kè	VO	to go to class; to start a class
13. 念	niàn	V	to read aloud
14. 課文	kèwén	N	text of a lesson
15. 錄音	lùyīn	N	sound recording
16. 男的	nán de		male
17. 帥	shuài	Adj	handsome

** Please note that the character zhēn (really) appears in two forms. "眞" is the printing form, and "真" is the hand-written form.

Dialogue II: *Pinyin*

(Lǐ Yǒu gēn Xiǎo Bái shuōhuà.)

Lǐ Yǒu: Xiǎo Bái, nǐ píngcháng lái de hěn zǎo, jīntiān zěnme [G6] lái de zhème wǎn?

Xiǎo Bái: Wǒ zuótiān yùxí Zhōngwén, bànyè yì diǎn cái [G3] shuì jiào, nǐ yě shuì de hěn wǎn ma?

Lǐ Yǒu: Wǒ zuótiān shí diǎn jiù [G3] shuì le. Yīnwèi Wáng Péng bāng wǒ liànxí Zhōngwén, suǒyǐ wǒ gōngkè zuò de hěn kuài.

Xiǎo Bái: Yǒu ge Zhōngguó péngyou zhēn [G2] hǎo.

(Shàng Zhōngwén kè)

Lǎoshī: Dàjiā zǎo [1], xiànzài wǒmen kāishǐ shàng kè. Dì-qī kè nǐmen dōu yùxí le ma?

Xuésheng: Yùxí le.

Lǎoshī   Lǐ Yǒu, qǐng nǐ niàn kèwén. ... ... Nǐ niàn de hěn hǎo. Nǐ zuótiān wǎnshang tīng lùyīn le ba?

Lǐ Yǒu: Wǒ méi tīng.

Xiǎo Bái: Dànshì tā de péngyou chángcháng bāngzhù tā.

Lǎoshī: Nǐ de péngyou shì Zhōngguórén ma?

Lǐ Yǒu: Shì de.

Xiǎo Bái: Tā shì yí ge nán de, hěn shuài [2], jiào Wáng Péng.

Complex vs. Simplified: *Examples*

問	學	幾	號	話	寫	難	筆	電	聽
问	学	几	号	话	写	难	笔	电	听

Dialogue II: *Chinese*

（李友跟小白說話）

李友：小白，你平常來得很早，今天怎麼(G6)來得
　　　這麼晚？

小白：我昨天預習中文，半夜一點才(G3)睡覺，你
　　　也睡得很晚嗎？

李友：我昨天十點就(G3)睡了。因為王朋幫我練習
　　　中文，所以我功課做得很快。

小白：有個中國朋友真(G2)好。

（上中文課）

老師：大家早(1)，現在我們開始上課。第七(G4)課
　　　你們都預習了嗎？

學生：預習了。

老師：李友，請你念課文。...你念得很好。你
　　　昨天晚上聽錄音了吧？

李友：我沒聽。

小白：但是她的朋友常常幫助她。

老師：你的朋友是中國人嗎？

李友：是的。

小白：他是一個男的，很帥(2)，叫王朋。

Notes:

(1) 早 (**Zǎo**, Good morning!), 早安 (**Zǎo ān**, Good morning!), and 你好 (**Nǐ hǎo**, How do you do?), may strike many Chinese speakers as rather formal and western, but they are gradually gaining acceptance among young and educated people.

(2) 帅 (**shuài**) is used to describe a handsome, usually young, man. To describe a pretty girl one uses the word 漂亮 (**piàoliang**, beautiful). The term 好看 (**hǎokàn**, good looking), is gender neutral. It can be used for both sexes.

On Chinese Characters

There are now two Chinese scripts in use, the so-called 繁體字 (fántǐzì, the complex or traditional script) and 簡體字 (jiǎntǐzì, the simplified script). In Taiwan, instead of 繁體字 (fántǐzì) the term 正體字 (zhèngtǐzì, the orthodox script) is used. In traditional China, one wrote vertically from the top to the bottom and from right to left. In Taiwan this practice is still alive, but one can also see articles or books that are printed horizontally from left to right. In mainland China everyone writes horizontally from left to right for practical purposes, and will write from the top to the bottom only to achieve some special aesthetic calligraphical effect.

Supplementary Vocabulary

1.	鉛筆	qiānbǐ	N	pencil
2.	鋼筆	gāngbǐ	N	fountain pen
3.	毛筆	máobǐ	N	writing brush
4.	紙	zhǐ	N	paper
5.	本子	běnzi	N	notebook
6.	午覺	wǔjiào	N	nap

GRAMMAR

1. Descriptive Complements (I)

The word 得 (de) can be used after a verb or an adjective. This lesson mainly deals with a verb followed by 得 (de). The part which comes after 得 (de) is called a descriptive complement, which can be an adjective, an adverb, or a verb phrase. In this lesson, the words that function as descriptive complements are all adjectives. These complements serve as comments on the actions.

(1) 他寫字寫得很好。

    Tā xiě zì xiě de hěn hǎo.

    (He writes characters well.)

    [很好(hěn hǎo, very good) is a comment on the action 寫(xiě, to write).]

(2) 他昨天睡覺睡得很晚。

    Tā zuótiān shuì jiào shuì de hěn wǎn.

    (He went to bed late last night.)

    [很晚 (hěn wǎn, very late) is a comment on the action 睡覺 (shuìjiào, to sleep).]

(3) 妹妹歌唱得很好。

    Mèimei gē chàng de hěn hǎo.

    (My younger sister sings beautifully.)

    [很好(hěn hǎo, very good) is a comment on the action 唱 (chàng, to sing).]

If what serves as a complement is an adjective, the adjective is usually preceded by 很(hěn, very), as in the case of an adjective used as a predicate. If the verb is followed by an object, the verb has to be repeated before it can be followed by the "得 (de) + Complement" structure, e.g., 寫字寫得 (xiě zì xiě de) in (1). By repeating the verb, the "verb + object" combination preceding it becomes a "topic" and the complement that follows serves as a comment on it. When both the listener and the speaker understand the context, the first verb can be omitted, as seen in (3).

2. 太 (tài, too) and 真 (zhēn, really)

When adverbs 太 (tài, too) and 真 (zhēn, really) are used in exclamatory sentences, they convey in most cases not new factual information but the speaker's approval, disapproval, or some other personal emotions. If the speaker wants to make a more "objective" statement or description, other intensifiers such as 很 (hěn, very), or 特別 (tèbié, especially) are often used in place of 太 (tài, too) or 真 (zhēn, really).

(1) A: 他寫字寫得怎麼樣？

    Tā xiě zì xiě de zěnmeyàng?

    (How well does he write characters?)

One would normally answer:

B: 他寫字寫得很好。

    Tā xiě zì xiě de hěn hǎo.

    (He writes characters very well.)

Rather than:

B1. **Incorrect:** 他寫字寫得真好。

    Tā xiě zì xiě de zhēn hǎo.

Compare "B1" with "C" below:

C: 小張：小李，你寫字寫得真好！ 你可以幫助我嗎？

    Xiǎo Zhāng: Xiǎo Lǐ, nǐ xiě zì xiě de zhēn hǎo! Nǐ kěyǐ bāngzhù wǒ ma?

    (Xiao Zhang: Xiao Li, you write characters really well! Will you help me?)

When 太 (tài, too) is used in an exclamation, 了 (le) usually appears at the end of the sentence:

(2) 這本書太有意思了！

    Zhè běn shū tài yǒu yìsi le!

    (This book is really interesting!)

(3) 我的語法太不好了！我得多練習。

    Wǒ de yǔfǎ tài bù hǎo le! Wǒ děi duō liànxí.

    (My grammar is indeed awful! I have to practice more.)

(4) 你跳舞跳得太好了。

    Nǐ tiào wǔ tiào de tài hǎo le!

    (You really dance beautifully!)

3. The Adverb 就 (jiù) (I)

The adverb 就 (jiù) is used before a verb to suggest the earliness, briefness, or quickness of the action.

(1) 他明天早上八點就得上課。

    Tā míngtiān zǎoshang bā diǎn jiù děi shàng kè.

    (He has to go to class [as early as] at 8 o'clock tomorrow morning.)

(2) 他昨天就來了。

    Tā zuótiān jiù lái le.

    (He came [as early as] yesterday.)

就 (jiù) and 才 (cái) compared [See also L.5 G6]

The adverb 就 (jiù) suggests the earliness or promptness of an action in the speaker's judgment, while the adverb 才 (cái) suggests tardiness or lateness of the action as perceived by the speaker.

(1) A: 八點上課，他七點就來了。

    Bā diǎn shàng kè, tā qī diǎn jiù lái le.

    (Class starts at eight, but he came [as early as] seven.)

   B: 八點上課，他八點半才來。

    Bā diǎn shàng kè, tā bā diǎn bàn cái lái.

    (Class started at eight, but he didn't come until 8:30.)

(2) A: 我昨天五點鐘就回家了。

    Wǒ zuótiān wǔ diǎnzhōng jiù huí jiā le.

    (Yesterday I went home when it was only five.)

   B: 我昨天五點才回家。

    Wǒ zuótiān wǔ diǎn cái huí jiā.

    (Yesterday I didn't go home until five o'clock.)

Note: When commenting on a past action, 就 (jiù) is always used with 了 (le) to indicate promptness, but not 才 (cái).

4. Ordinal Numbers

Ordinal numbers in Chinese are formed by placing 第 (dì) before the cardinal numbers, e.g., 第一 (dì-yī, the first) 、第二杯茶 (dì-èr bēi chá, the second cup of tea)、第三個月 (dì-sān ge yuè, the third month). . . . However, 第 is not used in names of months: 一月、二月、三月. . . . Neither is it used to indicate the seniority of brothers and sisters: 大哥、二哥、三哥. . . ; 大姐、二姐、三姐. . . .

5. 有一點兒 (yǒu yì diǎnr, somewhat; a little bit; kind of)

The phrase 有一點兒 (yǒu yì diǎn) precedes adjectives or verbs, indicating a slight degree. It often carries a negative or complaining tone. The 一 in the phrase can be optional.

(1) 我覺得中文有(一)點兒難。

Wǒ juéde Zhōngwén yǒu yì diǎnr nán.

(I think Chinese is a little bit difficult.)

(2) 我有(一)點兒不喜歡他。

Wǒ yǒu yì diǎnr bù xǐhuan tā.

(I sort of don't like him.)

(3) 我覺得這一課生詞有點兒多。

Wǒ juéde zhè yí kè shēngcí yǒu diǎnr duō.

(I think there are a bit too many new words in this lesson.)

Please do not confuse 有一點兒 (yǒu yì diǎnr, a little), which is an adverbial modifying an adjective, with 一點兒 (yì diǎnr, a little),which usually modifies a noun. In the above sentences, 有一點兒 (yǒu yì diǎnr) cannot be replaced by 一點兒 (yì diǎnr). Compare:

(4) 給我一點兒咖啡。

Gěi wǒ yì diǎnr kāfēi.

(Give me a little coffee.)

(5) 給我一點兒時間。

Gěi wǒ yì diǎnr shíjiān.

(Give me a little time.)

(6) 我有一點兒忙。

> Wǒ yǒu yì diǎnr máng.

> (I am kind of busy.)

(7) 她有一點兒不高興。

> Tā yǒu yìdiǎnr bù gāoxìng..

> (She is a little bit unhappy.)

6. 怎麼 (zěnme, how come) in Questions

怎麼 (zěnme, how come) is an interrogative adverb, which is often used in a question to ask about the manner, but sometimes it is used to ask about the reason or the cause as well.

(1) 你怎麼才來？已經下課了。

> Nǐ zěnme cái lái? Yǐjīng xià kè le.

> (How come you've just arrived? The class is over.)

(2) 你怎麼沒去看電影？

> Nǐ zěnme méi qù kàn diànyǐng?

> (Why didn't you go to the movie?)

(3) 怎麼，你不認識他？他不是你的老師嗎？

> Zěnme, nǐ bú rènshi tā? Tā bú shì nǐ de lǎoshī ma?

> (What? You don't know him? Isn't he your teacher?)

When 怎麼 (zěnme, how come) is used to ask about the cause or reason for something, it implies a surprise on the part of the speaker, while 爲什麼 (wèishénme, why), which is more commonly used to ask about the cause or reason, does not.

怎麼 (zěnme, how come) can stand alone as a clause, as in (3).

PATTERN DRILLS

A. Verb + 得 (de) + Complement

1. Tā kǎo	de	hěn hǎo.
2. Xiǎo Gāo zuótiān shuì		hěn wǎn.
3. Nàge xuésheng yùxí		búcuò.
4. Wǒ dìdi chī		hěn duō
5. Lǎoshī lái		hěn zǎo

1. 她考 　　　　　　　得 　　　　很好。
2. 小高昨天睡 　　　　　　　　　很晚。
3. 那個學生預習 　　　　　　　不錯。
4. 我弟弟吃 　　　　　　　　　很多。
5. 老師來 　　　　　　　　　　很早。

B. Verb + Object + Verb + 得 (de) + Complement

1. Wáng Péng shuō huà	shuō	de	hěn kuài.
2. Xiǎo Bái hē píjiǔ	hē		hěnduō.
3. Tā niàn kèwén	niàn		búcuò.
4. Wǒ xiě Zhōngguózì	xiě		bú tài hǎo.
5. Nǐ mèimei chàng gē	chàng		hěn hǎo.

1. 王朋說話 　　　說　　　得　　　很快。
2. 小白喝啤酒 　　　喝　　　　　　很多。
3. 他念課文 　　　念　　　　　　不錯。
4. 我寫中國字 　　　寫　　　　　　不太好。
5. 你妹妹唱歌 　　　唱　　　　　　很好。

C. 太 (tài, too)

1. Zhège zì	tài	nán.	le.
2. Wáng lǎoshī		máng	
3. Zhè yí kè de shēngcí		duō	

4. Wǒ de jiā	tài	xiǎo	le.
5. Nǐ		kèqi	
6. Zhège diànyǐng		yǒuyìsi	
7. Xiǎo Gāo de jiā		piàoliang	
8. Jīntiān de zhōngwén kè		róngyì	

1. 這個字 　　　　　 <u>太</u>　　難　　<u>了</u>。

2. 王老師 　　　　　　　　忙

3. 這一課的生詞 　　　　　多

4. 我的家 　　　　　　　　小

5. 你 　　　　　　　　　　客氣

6. 這個電影 　　　　　　　有意思

7. 小高的家 　　　　　　　漂亮

8. 今天的中文課 　　　　　容易

D. <u>有一點兒</u> (yǒu yìdiǎnr, a little bit) + Adjective

1. Jīntiān de yǔfǎ	yǒu yìdiǎnr	nán.
2. Dì wǔ kè de shēngcí		duō.
3. Wáng lǎoshī míngtiān		máng.
4. Wǔ diǎnzhōng chī wǎnfàn		zǎo.
5. Bànyè yī diǎn cái shuì jiào		wǎn.
6. Lǐ xiǎojie shuō huà		kuài.

1. 今天的語法 　　　<u>有一點兒</u>　　　難。

2. 第五課的生詞 　　　　　　　　　　多。

3. 王老師明天 　　　　　　　　　　　忙。

4. 五點鐘吃晚飯 　　　　　　　　　　早。

5. 半夜一點才睡覺 　　　　　　　　　晚。

6. 李小姐說話 　　　　　　　　　　　快。

E. 怎麼 (zěnme, how come)

1. Zuótiān de diànyǐng hěn hǎo,	nǐ zěnme	měi qù kàn?
2. Shí diǎn shàngkè,		shí diǎn bàn cái lái?
3. Zuótiān shì Xiǎo Gāo de shēngrì		méiyǒu lái?
4. Jīntiān de kǎoshì hěn róngyì		kǎo de zhème bù hǎo?
5. Míngtiān yǒu kǎoshì		méiyǒu fùxí.
6. Gāo Xiǎoyīn zài túshūguǎn gōngzuò		bú rènshi tā?
7. Bā diǎn bàn cái kāi huì		qī diǎn jiù lái le?
8. Jīntiān shì xīngqīyī		méi qù shàng kè

1. 昨天的電影很好 ， 　　你 怎麼　　　沒去看 ？

2. 十點上課 ，　　　　　　　　　　十點半才來 ？

3. 昨天是小高的生日　　　　　　　沒有來 ？

→ 4. 今天的考試很容易　　　　　　　考得這麼不好　 ？

5. 明天有考試　　　　　　　　　　沒有復習 ？

6. 高小音在圖書館工作　　　　　　不認識她 ？

7. 八點半才開會　　　　　　　　　七點就來了 ？

8. 今天是星期一　　　　　　　　　沒去上課 ？

今天我十二點鐘才吃晚

F. 才 (cái)

1. Māma hěn wǎn	cái	huílai.
2. Xiǎo Gāo shí diǎn		chī zǎofàn.
3. Wǒ gēge zuótiān wǎnshang bā diǎn		chī wǎnfàn.
4. Tā de tóngxué zuótiān bànyè		shuì jiào.
5. Bā diǎn bàn kǎoshì, tā jiǔ diǎn		lái.
6. Bàba jīntiān hěn máng, zhōumò		yǒukòngr.
7. Wǒ yào zài xuéxiào tīng lùyīn, wǔ diǎnzhōng		huí jiā.

1. 媽媽很晚　　　　　　　　才　　　回來 。

2. 小高十點　　　　　　　　　　　吃早飯 。

3. 我哥哥昨天晚上八點　　　　　　吃晚飯 。

4. 他的同學昨天半夜 　　 **才** 　　 睡覺。

5. 八點半考試，他九點 　　　　　　 來 。

6. 爸爸今天很忙，週末 　　　　　　 有空兒。

7. 我要在學校聽錄音，五點鐘 　　　　 回家。

G. **就** (jiù)

1. Wǒ zuótiān wǎnshang shí diǎn 　　　 **jiù** 　 shuì le.
2. Tā zǎoshang qī diǎn bàn 　　　　　　 kāishǐ fùxí kèwén le.
3. Xiǎo Wáng zǎoshang wǔ diǎn 　　　　 qù xuéxiào le.
4. Tā chīfàn yǐhòu 　　　　　　　　　 qù túshūguǎn kàn shū le.
5. Jiǔ diǎn kǎoshì, Xiǎo Bái bā diǎn 　　 lái le.
6. Tā píngcháng liù diǎn chī wǎnfàn, jīntiān wǔ diǎn 　 chī le.

1. 我昨天晚上十點 　　　　　　 **就** 　 睡了。

2. 他早上七點半 　　　　　　　　 開始復習課文了。

3. 小王早上五點 　　　　　　　　 去學校了。

4. 她吃飯以後 　　　　　　　　　 去圖書館看書了。

5. 九點考試，小白八點 　　　　　 來了。

6. 他平常六點吃晚飯，今天五點 　 吃了。

H. **真** (zhēn, really)

1. Zhège xuéxiào 　　　 **zhēn** 　　 hǎo.
2. Jīntiān de fàn 　　　　　　　　 bù hǎo chī.
3. Wáng lǎoshī 　　　　　　　　　 máng.
4. Zhège zì 　　　　　　　　　　　 nán.
5. Nǐ de Zhōngwén 　　　　　　　 búcuò.
6. Zhè yí kè de yǔfǎ 　　　　　　 róngyì.
7. Zhège diànyǐng 　　　　　　　 yǒu yìsi.
8. Zuótiān de gōngkè 　　　　　　 duō.

1. 這個學校　　　　　　　真　　　好。
2. 今天的飯　　　　　　　　　　不好吃。
3. 王老師　　　　　　　　　　　忙。
4. 這個字　　　　　　　　　　　難。
5. 你的中文　　　　　　　　　　不錯。
6. 這一課的語法　　　　　　　　容易。
7. 這個電影　　　　　　　　　　有意思。
8. 昨天的功課　　　　　　　　　多。

( )

( )

( )

( )

Review Dialogue I and number the pictures above in the correct order.

ENGLISH TEXT

Dialogue I

(Wang Peng is talking with Li You.)

Wang Peng: How did you do on last week's exam?

Li You: Pretty well. Because you helped me review, I did pretty well, but the teacher said I was too slow in writing the Chinese characters.

Wang Peng: Really? I'll practice writing characters with you from now on. I'll teach you how to write Chinese characters. How is that?

Li You: That would be great! Let's do it right now. Here's a pen.

Wang Peng: OK, I'll teach you how to write the character "nán (difficult)".

Li You: You write characters really well, and fast, too.

Wang Peng: You flatter me. Do you have Chinese tomorrow?

Li You: Yes. Tomorrow we'll study Lesson Seven.

Wang Peng: Have you prepared it?

Li You: Yes. I have. The grammar in Lesson Seven is very easy. I can understand all of it, but there are too many new words, and the Chinese characters are rather difficult, too.

Wang Peng: Let me practice with you tonight.

Li You: Great. Thank you.

Wang Peng: Don't mention it. See you tonight.

Dialogue II

(Li You is talking with Xiao Bai.)

Li You: Xiao Bai, you usually come very early. How come you got here so late today?

Xiao Bai: Yesterday I was preparing Chinese. I didn't go to bed till one o'clock. Did you go to bed very late, too?

Li You: No, yesterday I went to bed at ten. Because Wang Peng helped me practice Chinese, I finished my homework very quickly.

Xiao Bai: It's great to have a Chinese friend.

(In the Chinese class)

Teacher: Good morning, everyone. Let's begin. Have you all prepared Lesson Seven?

Students: Yes, we have.

Teacher: Li You, would you please read the text aloud? ...You read very well. Did you listen to the tape recording last night?

Li You: No, I didn't.

Xiao Bai: But her friend often helps her.

Teacher: Is your friend Chinese?

Li You: Yes.

Xiao Bai: It's a he. He is really handsome. His name is Wang Peng.

漢字復習

1. Write 1-10 in Chinese.

2. Write as many radicals as you can remember. Give also their *pinyin* and meanings.

3. Write as many two-stroke characters as you can.

4. Write as many characters as you can with the element 人 in them.

5. Write at least five characters with the element 女 in them.

6. Write ten or more characters with the element 口 in them.

7. Write two characters which are pronounced as nán.

8. Write as many words as you can that are related to food.

9. Write as many words as you can that are related to time.

10. Write as many verbs as you can.

Lesson Eight   School Life
第八課　　學校生活

A DIARY: *A TYPICAL SCHOOL DAY*

Vocabulary

1. 篇	piān	M	(a measure word for essays, articles, etc.)
2. 日記	rìjì	N	diary
3. 早上	zǎoshang	T	morning
4. 起床	qǐ chuáng	VO	to get up
床	chuáng	N	bed
5. 洗澡	xǐ zǎo	VO	to take a bath/shower

不知

餐廳

6.	早飯	zǎofàn	N	breakfast
7.	一邊…一邊	yìbiān…yìbiān		(indicates two simultaneous actions)
8.	教室	jiàoshì	N	classroom
9.	發音	fāyīn	N	pronunciation
10.	新	xīn	Adj	new
11.	電腦	diànnǎo	N	computer
	腦	nǎo	N	brain
12.	中午	zhōngwǔ	N	noon
13.	餐廳	cāntīng	N	dining room; cafeteria
14.	午飯 中飯	wǔfàn	N	lunch
15.	報	bào	N	newspaper
16.	宿舍	sùshè	N	dormitory
17.	到	dào	V	to arrive
18.	那兒	nàr	Pr	there
19.	…的時候	…de shíhou		when…; at the time of…
20.	正在	zhèngzài	Adv	in the middle of (doing something)
21.	以前	yǐqián	T	before; ago; previously
22.	告訴	gàosu	V	to tell
23.	已經	yǐjīng	Adv	already

炎　發音

A Diary: *Pinyin*

Lǐ Yǒu de yì piān rìjì

Bāyuè jiǔrì, xīngqīyī

Wǒ jīntiān zǎoshang qī diǎn bàn qǐchuáng (G1), xǐle zǎo yǐhòu jiù (G2) chī zǎofàn. Wǒ yìbiān chī fàn, yìbiān (G3) tīng lùyīn. Jiǔ diǎnzhōng dào jiàoshì qù shàng kè (G4).

Dì yī jié kè shì Zhōngwén, lǎoshī jiāo wǒmen fāyīn (G5), shēngcí hé yǔfǎ, yě jiāo wǒmen xiě zì, hái gěile (G6) wǒmen yì piān xīn kèwén, zhè piān kèwén hěn yǒu yìsi. Dì èr jié kè shì diànnǎo kè, hěn nán. Zhōngwǔ wǒ hé tóngxuémen yìqǐ dào cāntīng qù chī wǔfàn. Wǒmen yìbiān chī, yìbiān liànxí shuō Zhōngwén. Xiàwǔ wǒ dào túshūguǎn qù kàn bào. Sì diǎnzhōng Wáng Péng lái zhǎo wǒ qù dǎ qiú. Wǔ diǎn sān kè chī wǎnfàn. Qī diǎn bàn wǒ qù Xiǎo Bái de sùshè gēn tā liáo tiān(r). Dào nàr de shíhou, tā zhèngzài (G7) zuò gōngkè. Wǒ bā diǎn bàn huí jiā. Shuì jiào yǐqián, gěi Wáng Péng dǎle yí ge diànhuà, gàosù tā míngtiān yào kǎoshì. Tā shuō tā yǐjīng zhīdao le.

A Diary: *Chinese*

李友的一篇日記

八月九日　　星期一

我今天早上七點半起床^(G1)，洗了澡以後就^(G2)吃早飯。我一邊吃飯，一邊^(G3)聽錄音。九點鐘到教室去上課^(G4)。

第一節課是中文，老師教我們發音^(G5)、生詞和語法，也教我們寫字，還給了^(G6)我們一篇新課文，這篇課文很有意思。第二節課是電腦課，很難。中午我和同學們一起到餐廳去吃午飯。我們一邊吃，一邊練習說中文。下午我到圖書館去看報。四點鐘王朋來找我去打球。五點三刻吃晚飯。七點半我去小白的宿舍跟他聊天(兒)。到那兒的時候，他正在^(G7)做功課。我八點半回家。睡覺以前，給王朋打了一個電話，告訴他明天要考試。他說他已經知道了。

Can you find the sentence in the text above which depicts the scene on the left side?

Go back to the last page and find the sentence depicting the picture on the left.

A LETTER: *TALKING ABOUY STUDYING CHINESE*

Vocabulary

1.	封	fēng	M	(a measure word for letters)
2.	信	xìn	N	letter
3.	最近	zuìjìn	T	recently
	最	zuì		(indicator for the superlative degree); most
	近	jìn		near
4.	學期	xuéqī	N	school term; semester/quarter
5.	除了...以外	chúle...yǐwài	Conj	in addition to; besides [See G8]
6.	專業	zhuānyè	N	major; specialty
7.	會	huì	AV	can; know how to [See G9]
8.	開始	kāishǐ	N/V	in the beginning; to begin; to start
9.	習慣	xíguàn	V	to be accustomed to
10.	後來	hòulái	T	later
11.	清楚	qīngchu	Adj	clear
12.	進步	jìnbù	V	to make progress
13.	音樂會	yīnyuèhuì	N	concert

14.	希望	xīwàng	V	to hope
15.	能	néng	AV	can, able to
16.	用	yòng	V/N	to use/use (See L. 16)
17.	笑	xiào	V	to laugh; to laugh at
18.	祝	zhù	V	to wish

Proper Nouns

| 19. | 意文 | Yìwén | N | (a given name) |

A Letter: *Pinyin*

Yì fēng xìn

Zhāng xiǎojie:

Nǐ hǎo! Hǎo jiǔ bú jiàn, zuìjìn zěnmeyàng?

Zhège xuéqī wǒ hěn máng, <u>chúle</u> zhuānyè kè <u>yǐwài</u>, hái ^(G8) děi xué Zhōngwén. Wǒmen de Zhōngwén kè hěn yǒu yìsi. Yīnwei wǒmen de Zhōngwén lǎoshī zhǐ <u>huì</u>^(G9) shuō Zhōngwén, bú huì shuō Yīngwén, suǒyǐ shàngkè de shíhou wǒmen zhǐ shuō Zhōngwén, bù shuō Yīngwén. Kāishǐ wǒ bù xíguàn, hòulái, wǒ yǒule yí ge Zhōngguó péngyou, tā shuō huà shuō de hěn qīngchu, chángcháng gēn wǒ yìqǐ liànxí shuō Zhōngwén, suǒyǐ wǒ de Zhōngwén jìnbù de hěn kuài.

Nǐ xǐhuan tīng yīnyuè ma? Xià xīngqīliù, wǒmen xuéxiào yǒu yí ge yīnyuèhuì, xīwàng nǐ <u>néng</u> ^(G9) lái. Wǒ yòng Zhōngwén xiě xìn xiě de hěn bù hǎo, qǐng bié xiào wǒ.   Zhù

Hǎo

Nǐ de péngyou

Yìwén

Bāyuè shírì

A Letter: *Chinese*

一封信

張小姐：

　　你好！好久不見，最近怎麼樣？

　　這個學期我很忙，除了專業課以外，還(G8)得學中文。我們的中文課很有意思。因為我們的中文老師只會(G9)說中文，不會說英文，所以上課的時候我們只說中文，不說英文。開始我不習慣，後來，我有了一個中國朋友，他說話說得很清楚，常常跟我一起練習說中文，所以我的中文進步得很快。

　　你喜歡聽音樂嗎？下星期六，我們學校有一個音樂會，希望你能(G9)來。我用中文寫信寫得很不好，請別笑我。祝

好

　　　　　　　　　　　　　　你的朋友

　　　　　　　　　　　　　　　意文

　　　　　　　　　　　　　　八月十日

GRAMMAR

1. The Position of Time-When Expressions

The time-when expressions of time should go before the verb, e.g.:

(1) 我們十點上課。

Wǒmen shí diǎn shàng kè.

(We have class at ten.)

(2) 我們幾點鐘去？

Wǒmen Jǐ diǎnzhōng qù?

(What time should we go?)

(3) 你什麼時候睡覺？

Nǐ shénme shíhou shuì jiào?

(What time do you go to bed?)

(4) 他明天上午八點來。

Tā míngtiān shàngwǔ bā diǎn lái.

(He will come at eight tomorrow morning.)

2. 就 (jiù) (II) [See also L.7 G3]

The adverb 就 (jiù) can also connect two verbal phrases and suggest that the second action happens as soon as the first one is completed.

(1) 他今天早上起床以後就聽中文錄音。

Tā jīntiān zǎoshang qǐchuáng yǐhòu jiù tīng Zhōngwén lùyīn.

(He listened to his Chinese tapes right after he got up this morning.)

(2) 寫了信以後就去睡覺。

Xiěle xìn yǐhòu jiù qù shuì jiào.

(Go to bed right after you finish writing the letter.)

(3) 我做了功課以後就去朋友家玩。

Wǒ zuòle gōngkè yǐhòu jiù qù péngyou jiā wán.

(I will go to my friend's right after I have done my homework.)

3. 一邊...一邊... (yìbiān...yìbiān...)

This structure denotes the simultaneity of two ongoing actions. Usually, the word/phrase for the action that started earlier follows the first 一邊 (yìbiān), while the word/phrase for the action that started later follows the second 一邊 (yìbiān).

(1) 我們一邊吃飯，一邊練習說中文。

Wǒmen yìbiān chī fàn, yìbiān liànxí shuō Zhōngwén.

(We practiced speaking Chinese while having dinner.)

(2) 他常常一邊吃飯一邊看電視。

Tā chángcháng yìbiān chī fàn yìbiān kàn diànshì.

(He often watches T.V. while eating.)

Sometimes, the action denoted by the word/phrase following the second 一邊 (yìbiān) can be somewhat more important, while the first 一邊 (yìbiān) precedes the action which provides a background.

(3) 我一邊唱歌一邊寫字。

Wǒ yìbiān chàng gē, yìbiān xiě zì.

(I sing while writing characters.)

(4) 我妹妹喜歡一邊聽音樂一邊看書。

Wǒ mèimei xǐhuan yìbiān tīng yīnyuè, yìbiān kàn shū.

(My younger sister loves reading while listening to music.)

4. Serial Verbs/Verb Phrases

A number of verbs or verb phrases can be used in succession to represent a series of actions. The sequential order of the verbs or verb phrases usually tallies with the temporal order of the actions. That is to say, what happens earlier in time is expressed earlier in the sentence.

(1) 他常常去餐廳吃飯。

Tā chángcháng qù cāntīng chī fàn.

(He often goes to the cafeteria to eat.)

(2) 下午我要到圖書館去看書。

Xiàwǔ wǒ yào dào túshūguǎn qù kàn shū.

(This afternoon I want to go to the library to read.)

(3) 我想找同學去打球。

    Wǒ xiǎng zhǎo tóngxué qù dǎ qiú.

    (I'd like to find some classmates to play ball with me.)

(4) 你明天來我家吃晚飯吧。

    Nǐ míngtiān lái wǒ jiā chī wǎnfàn ba.

    (Come and have dinner at my home tomorrow.)

Sometimes the first verb indicates the means or manner of the action.

(5) 他常常用中文寫信。

    Tā chángcháng yòng Zhōngwén xiě xìn.

    (He often writes letters in Chinese.)

5. Double Objects

Some verbs can take two objects, with the object which represents a person or persons preceding the one which represents an inanimate thing.

(1) 老師教我們發音、生詞和語法。

    Lǎoshī jiāo wǒmen fāyīn, shēngcí hé yǔfǎ.

    (The teacher teaches us pronunciation, vocabulary and grammar.)

(2) 哥哥給了我一張照片。

    Gēge gěile wǒ yì zhāng zhàopiàn.

    (My brother gave me a photo.)

(3) 你教我電腦，可以嗎？

    Nǐ jiāo wǒ diànnǎo, kěyǐ ma?

    (Teach me how to use a computer, will you?)

(4) 我想問你一個問題。

    Wǒ xiǎng wèn nǐ yí ge wèntí.

    (I'd like to ask you a question.)

6. More on the Particle 了 (le) (II) [See also L.5 G5 and L.10 G2]

If a statement enumerates a series of realized actions or events, usually 了 (le) is used at the end of the series, rather than after each of the verbs.

昨天第一節課是中文。老師教我們發音、生詞和語法，也教我們寫字，還給了我們一篇<u>閱讀</u>課文。這篇課文很有意思。

Zuótiān dì-yī jié kè shì Zhōngwén. Lǎoshī jiāo wǒmen fāyīn, shēngcí hé yǔfǎ, yě jiāo wǒmen xiězì, hái gěile wǒmen yì piān <u>yuèdú</u> kèwén. Zhè piān kèwén hén yǒu yìsi.

(The first class was Chinese. The teacher taught us pronunciation, vocabulary and grammar. He/she taught us how to write the characters, and gave us a <u>reading</u> text. That text was very interesting.)

7. <u>. . . 的時候，正在. . .</u> (...de shíhou, zhèngzài..., when...be doing...)

This structure expresses the ongoing process of an action at a certain point of time.

(1) 我到他宿舍的時候，他正在做功課。

Wǒ dào tā sùshè de shíhou, tā zhèngzài zuò gōngkè.

(When I got to his dorm, he was doing his homework.)

(2) 老師到教室的時候，我們正在看書。

Lǎoshī dào jiàoshì de shíhou, wǒmen zhèngzài kàn shū.

(When the teacher came into the classroom, we were reading.)

(3) 我進他的宿舍的時候，他正在聽音樂。

Wǒ jìn tā de sùshè de shíhou, tā zhèngzài tīng yīnyuè.

(When I entered his dorm, he was listening to music.)

(4) 我給他打電話的時候，他正在練習發音。

Wǒ gěi tā dǎ diànhuà de shíhou, tā zhèngzài liànxí fāyīn.

(When I called him, he was practicing pronunciation.)

8. <u>除了. . . 以外, 還</u> (chúle...yǐwài, hái, in addition to..., also...)

(1) 我除了學中文以外，還學日文。

Wǒ chúle xué Zhōngwén yǐwài, hái xué Rìwén.

(Besides Chinese, I also study Japanese.)

(2) 上個週末我們除了看電影以外，還聽了音樂。

Shàngge zhōumò wǒmen chúle kàn diànyǐng yǐwài, hái tīngle yīnyuè.

(Last weekend besides seeing a movie we also listened to some music.)

(3) 他除了喜歡聽音樂以外，還喜歡打球。

Tā chúle xǐhuan tīng yīnyuè yǐwài, hái xǐhuan dǎ qiú.

(In addition to listening to music, he also likes to play ball.)

9. 能 (néng) 會 (huì) (I) Compared

Both 能 and 會 have many meanings. In this lesson, 能 means having the capacity or conditions for doing something.

(1) 我能喝十杯啤酒。

Wǒ néng hē shí bēi píjiǔ.

(I can drink ten glasses of beer.)

(2) 今天下午我要開會，不能去聽音樂。

Jīntiān xiàwǔ wǒ yào kāi huì, bù néng qù tīng yīnyuè.

(I have a meeting this afternoon, and I cannot go to listen to music.)

(3) 我的宿舍沒有電話，所以不能打電話。

Wǒ de sùshè méiyǒu diànhuà, suǒyǐ bù néng dǎ diànhuà.

(There's no phone in my dorm, so I cannot make a phone call.)

(4) 小張會說英文。

Xiǎo Zhāng huì shuō yīngwén.

(Little Zhang speaks English.)

(5) 李友會唱很多美國歌。

Lǐ Yǒu huì chàng hěnduō Měiguó gē.

(Li You can sing many American songs.)

(6) 誰會打球？

Shéi huì dǎ qiú?

(Who can play ball?)

會 (huì), as used in this lesson, means being able to do something as a result of a process of learning. However, referring to particular language skills, 能 (néng) is often used, as in the sentence 我能用中文寫信 (Wǒ néng yòng Zhōngwén xiě xìn. I can write letters in Chinese.)

PATTERN DRILLS

A. Time Expression + V

Example: Wǒmen shàngwǔ jiǔ diǎn shàngkè. (qī diǎn bàn qǐchuáng)
---> Wǒmen qī diǎn bàn qǐchuáng.

我們上午九點上課。（七點半，起床）

--> 我們七點半起床。

1. Wáng Péng wǎnshang shí diǎn shuì jiào. (shàngwǔ bā diǎn, shàng kè)
2. Wǒmen shàng kè yǐqián yùxí kèwén. (huí jiā yǐqián, tīng lùyīn)
3. Wǒde péngyou míngtiān xiàwǔ lái. (míngtiān shàngwǔ, lái)
4. Xià kè yǐhòu, wǒ xiǎng qù dǎ qiú. (wǎnfàn yǐhòu, kàn diànyǐng)
5. Wǒ huí jiā yǐqián gēn péngyou liáo tiān. (shàng kè yǐqián, liànxí Zhōngwén)
6. Nǐ shénme shíhou kàn diànyǐng? (jǐ diǎnzhōng, kǎoshì)
7. Wǒ shí'ěr diǎn bàn dào cāntīng chī fàn. (liǎngdiǎn, dào túshūguǎn kàn shū)

1. 王朋昨天晚上十點睡覺。 （上午八點，上課）

2. 我們上課以前預習課文。 （回家以前，聽錄音）

3. 我的朋友明天下午來。 （明天上午，來）

4. 下課以後，我想去打球。 （晚飯以後，看電影）

5. 我回家以前跟朋友聊天。 （上課以前，練習中文）

6. 你什麼時候看電影？ （幾點鐘，考試）

7. 我十二點半到餐廳吃飯。 （兩點，到圖書館看書）

B. 一邊...一邊... (yìbiān...yìbiān...)

Example: Wǒ dìdi zuò gōngkè kàn diànshì
---> Wǒ dìdi yìbiān zuò gōngkè yìbiān kàn diànshì.

我弟弟 做功課 看電視

--> 我弟弟一邊做功課一邊看電視。

1. Wǒ mèimei chángcháng	chī fàn	shuō huà
2. Wang xiānsheng chángcháng	xǐ zǎo	chàng gē
3. Wǒ dìdi xǐhuan	xiě hànzì	tīng lùyīn.
4. Xiǎo Gāo yǒushíhòu	kàn bào	hē kāfēi
5. Wǒ hé Lǎo Lǐ	liáo tiānr	hē kělè
6. Tāmen	chī wǔfàn	liànxí shuō Zhōngwén
7. Wǒ gēn wǒde tóngxué	dǎ qiú	liáo tiānr.
8 . Wáng Péng hé Lǐ Yǒu	hē chá	tīng yīnyuè

1.我妹妹常常	吃飯	説話
2.王先生常常	洗澡	唱歌
3.我弟弟喜歡	寫漢字	聽錄音
4. 小高有時候	看報	喝咖啡
5.我和老李	聊天兒	喝可樂
6.他們	吃午飯	練習説中文
7.我跟我的同學	打球	聊天兒
8.王朋和李友	喝茶	聽音樂

C. Subject + Verb 1+ Verb 2

Example: Wáng Péng qù xuéxiào shàng kè. (dào Xiǎo Gāo jiā, chī fàn)
         ---> Wáng Péng dào Xiǎo Gāo jiā chī fàn.

    王朋去學校上課。（到小高家，吃飯）
    --> 王朋到小高家吃飯。

1. Wǒ dìdi chángcháng dào péngyou jiā kàn diànshì. (qù túshūguǎn, kàn shū)
2. Tā xǐhuan qù túshūguǎn kàn bào.   (qù jiàoshì, liànxí fāyīn)
3. Xiàkè yǐhòu tā qù zhǎo Wáng Péng dǎ qiú.   (qù, zhǎo péngyou liáo tiānr)
4. Tā gēn péngyou qù xuéxiào tīng lùyīn.   (qù lǎoshī jiā, wèn wèntí)
5. Wǒ de tóngxué yào lái wǒjiā wánr.   (lái wǒmen xuéxiào kàn diànyǐng)

1. 我弟弟常常到朋友家看電視。（去圖書館，看書）
2. 他喜歡去圖書館看報。　　　（去教室，練習發音）
3. 下課以後他去找王朋打球。　（去，找朋友，聊天兒）
4. 她跟朋友去學校聽錄音。　　（去老師家，問問題）
5. 我的同學要來我家玩兒。　　（來我們學校，看電影）

D. Verb + Object 1 + Object 2

D1:

1. Lǎoshī	jiāo	xuésheng	shēngcí.
2.		xuésheng	hànzì.
3.		Lǐyǒu	Zhōngwén.
4.		Xiǎo Bái	fāyīn.

D1:

1. 老師	教	學生	生詞
2.		學生	漢字
3.		李友	中文
4.		小白	發音

D2:

1. Wǒ de péngyou	gěi	lǎoshī	yì piān rìjì.
2.		tā dìdi	yí ge diànnǎo.
3.		lǎoshī	yì fēng xìn.
4.		tā bàba	yì zhāng zhàopiàn.
5.		wǒ	yì běn shū.
6.		Xiǎo Gāo	yìbēi kělè.

D2:

1. 我的朋友	給	老師	一篇日記。
2.		他弟弟	一個電腦。
3.		老師	一封信。

4. 我的朋友   給   他爸爸   一張照片。

5.   我   一本書。

6.   小高   一杯可樂。

E.   ...的時候，正在... (... de shíhou, zhèngzài ...)

1. Wǒ huí jiā	de shíhou	dìdi	zhèngzài	kàn diànshì.
2. Wǒmen dǎ qiú		Lǐ Yǒu gēn péngyou		shuō huà.
3. Wǒ qù tā sùshè		tā		kàn diànshì.
4. Wáng Péng gěi dìdi dǎ diànhuà		tā dìdi		shuì jiào.
5. Wǒ liànxí Zhōngwén		Xiǎo Gāo		dǎ qiú.
6. Wǒ gēn péngyou liáo tiānr		Xiǎo Bái		zuò gōngkè.
7. Lǎoshī dào túshūguǎn		wǒmen		kàn shū.
8. Lǐ Yǒu qù zhǎo Wáng Péng		Wáng Péng		yùxí gōngkè.

1. 我回家   的時候   弟弟   正在   看電視。

2. 我們打球   李友   跟朋友說話。

3. 我去他宿舍   他   看電視。

4. 王朋給弟弟打電話   他弟弟   睡覺。

5. 我練習中文   小高   打球。

6. 我跟朋友聊天兒   小白   做功課。

7. 老師到圖書館   我們   看書。

8. 李友去找王朋   王朋   預習功課。

F. 除了...以外，還... (chúle ... yǐwài, hái...)

1. Tā	chúle	tīng lùyīn	yǐwài, hái	niàn kèwén.
2		xué Yīngwén		xué Zhōngwén.
3.		huì shuō Zhōngwén		huì yòng Zhōngwén xiěxìn.
4.		shì wǒ de lǎoshī		shì wǒ de péngyou.
5.		hē kělè		hē píjiǔ.
6.		xǐhuan tīng yīnyuè		xǐhuan tiào wǔ.

1. 他　除了　　　聽錄音　　以外，還　　念課文。
2. 　　　　　　　學英文　　　　　　　學中文。
3. 　　　　　　　會説中文　　　　　　會用中文寫信。
4. 　　　　　　　是我的老師　　　　　是我的朋友。
5. 　　　　　　　喝可樂　　　　　　　喝啤酒。
6. 　　　　　　　喜歡聽音樂　　　　　喜歡跳舞。

G. 用 + Object + Verb + Object

1. Wǒmen	yòng	Zhōngwén	xiě rìjì.
2. Xiǎo Gāo		Yīngwén	gěi tā gēge xiě xìn.
3. Wǒ de tóngxué		diànnǎo	liànxí fāyīn.
4. Wǒ bàba		píjiǔbēi	hē chá.

1. 我們　　　　　　用　　中文　　寫日記。
2. 小高　　　　　　　　　英文　　給他哥哥寫信。
3. 我的同學　　　　　　　電腦　　練習發音。
4. 我爸爸　　　　　　　　啤酒杯　喝茶。

Can you describe what Li You did yesterday?

Don't forget to mention the time!

ENGLISH TEXT

An Entry in Li You's Diary

August 9, Monday

I got up at seven thirty this morning. After a shower I had breakfast. While I was eating, I listened to the tape recording. I went to the classroom at nine o'clcok.

The first period was Chinese. The teacher taught us pronunciation, new vocabulary, and grammar. (He/she) also taught us how to write Chinese characters, and gave us a new text. The text was very interesting. The second period was Computer Science. It's very difficult. At noon I went to the cafeteria with my classmates for lunch. While we were eating, we practiced speaking Chinese. In the afternoon I went to the library to read newspapers. At four o'clock Wang Peng came looking for me to play ball. I had dinner at a quarter to six. At seven thirty I went to Xiao Bai's dorm for a chat. When I got there, he was doing his homework. I got home at eight thirty. Before I went to bed, I gave Wang Peng a call. I told him there'd be an exam tomorrow. He said he already knew that.

A Letter

August 10

Dear Miss Zhang,

How are you? Long time no see. How are things recently?

This semester I'm very busy. Besides the classes required for my major, I also need to study Chinese. Our Chinese class is really interesting. Because our Chinese teacher can only speak Chinese and does not know how to speak English, in the class we speak only Chinese, no English. At the beginning I wasn't used to that. Then I made a Chinese friend. He speaks very clearly, and often speaks Chinese with me. As a result I have made a lot of progress with my Chinese.

Do you like to listen to music? Next Saturday there will be a concert in our school. I hope you can come. I do not write well in Chinese. Please don't laugh at me.

Best wishes

Your friend,

Yiwen

Lesson Nine Shopping
第九課 買東西

他一定很愛你 愛

DIALOGUE I: *BUYING CLOTHING*

買 愛

Vocabulary

1. 買	mǎi	V	to buy
2. 東西	dōngxi	N	things; objects
3. 售貨員	shòuhuòyuán	N	shop assistant
4. 要	yào	AV	have a desire for [see G1]
5. 衣服	yīfu	N	clothes
6. 件	jiàn	M	(a measure word for shirts, things, etc.)

sow for 元

163

7.	襯衫	chènshān	N	shirt
8.	顏色	yánsè	N	color
9.	黃 (黄)	huáng	Adj	yellow
10.	紅	hóng	Adj	red
11.	穿	chuān	V	to wear; to put on
12.	條	tiáo	M	(a measure word for pants and long, thin objects)
13.	褲子	kùzi	N	pants
14.	號	hào	N	number; size
15.	中	zhōng	Adj	medium
16.	貴	guì	Adj	expensive
17.	便宜	piányi	Adj	cheap; inexpensive
18.	付錢	fù qián	VO	to pay money
	錢	qián	N	money
19.	這兒	zhèr	Pr	here
20.	一共	yígòng	Adv	altogether
21.	多少	duōshao	QW	how much; how many
22.	塊	kuài	M	(the basic monetary unit); dollar
23.	毛	máo	M	(a fractional monetary unit, =1/10 of a kuai); dime
24.	分	fēn	M	(a fractional monetary unit, =1/100 of a kuai); cent
25.	百	bǎi	Nu	hundred
26.	找 (錢)	zhǎo(qián)	V	to give change [See also L.4]

Dialogue I: *Pinyin*

(Mǎi dōngxi)

Shòuhuòyuán: Xiǎojie [1], nín yào [G1] mǎi shénme yīfu?

Lǐ xiǎojie: Wǒ xiǎng mǎi yí jiàn [G2] chènshān.

Shòuhuòyuán: Nín xǐhuan shénme yánsè de [G3], huáng de háishi hóng de?

Lǐ xiǎojie: Wǒ xǐhuan chuān hóng de. Wǒ hái xiǎng mǎi yì tiáo kùzi.

Shòuhuòyuán: Duō [G4] dà de? Dà hào, zhōng hào háishi xiǎo hào de?

Lǐ xiǎojie: Zhōng hào de. Bú yào tài guì de, yě bú yào tài piányi [2] de.

Shòuhuòyuán: Zhè tiáo kùzi hé zhè jiàn chènshān zěnmeyàng?

Lǐ xiǎojie: Hěn hǎo, zài nǎr fùqián?

Shòuhuòyuán: Zài zhèr.

Lǐ xiǎojie: Yígòng duōshao qián?

Shòuhuòyuán: Chènshān èrshí kuài wǔ, kùzi sānshí'èr kuài jiǔ máo jiǔ,

                     yígòng shì wǔshísān kuài sì máo jiǔ fēn [G5].

Lǐ xiǎojie: Hǎo, zhè shì yìbǎi kuài qián.

Shòuhuòyuán: Zhǎo nín sìshíliù kuài wǔ máo yì. Xièxie.

Dialogue I: *Chinese*

（買東西）

售貨員：小姐[1]，您要[G1]買什麼衣服？

李小姐：我想買一件[G2]襯衫。

售貨員：您喜歡什麼顏色的[G3]，黃的還是紅的？

李小姐：我喜歡穿紅的。我還想買一條[G2]褲子。

售貨員：多[G4]大的？大號、中號還是小號的？

李小姐：中號的。不要太貴的，也不要太便宜[2]
　　　　的。

售貨員：這條褲子和這件襯衫怎麼樣？

李小姐：很好，在哪兒付錢？

售貨員：在這兒。

李小姐：一共多少錢？

售貨員：襯衫二十塊五，褲子三十二塊九毛九，
　　　　一共是五十三塊四毛九分[G5]。

李小姐：好，這是一百塊錢。

售貨員：找您四十六塊五毛一。謝謝。

Notes:

(1) In mainland China and Taiwan one addresses a salesperson as 小姐 (xiǎojie, Miss) or 先生 (xiānsheng, Mr.), as the case may be. Although the terms, 同志 (tóngzhì, comrade) and 師傅 (shīfu, lit. master, a skilled worker, usually used when addressing a male salesperson) are still used by older people in the Chinese inland, they are gradually

being replaced by the more fashionable 小姐 (xiǎojie, Miss) and 先生 (xiānsheng, Mr.), especially in coastal areas.

(2) 便 (pián) in 便宜 (piányi) is pronounced "pián," different from 便 (biàn) in 方便 (fangbiàn), which is pronounced "biàn." It is not uncommon in Chinese that the same character is pronounced differently and carries different meanings.

DIALOGUE II: *EXCHANGING SHOES*

Vocabulary

1.	雙	shuāng	M	a pair
2.	鞋	xié	N	shoes
3.	換	huàn	V	to change; to exchange (something for something else)
4.	一樣	yíyàng	Adj	same; alike
5.	雖然	suīrán	Conj	although
6.	大小	dàxiǎo	N	size
7.	合適	héshì	Adj	suitable
8.	咖啡色	kāfēisè	N	coffee color; brown
9.	黑	hēi	Adj	black
10.	不用	bú yòng	CE	need not

No Taxing and No Tipping in China

There is no sales tax for food or clothes in mainland China. It is also not customary to tip in a restaurant, although fancier restaurants often charge a service fee. In Taiwan consumers have to pay 商品稅 (shāngpǐn shuì, commodity tax).

Dialogue II: *Pinyin*

Lǐ xiǎojie: Duìbuqǐ, zhè shuāng xié tài xiǎo le. Néng bu néng huàn
                    yì shuāng?

Shòuhuòyuán: Méi wèntí. Nín kàn, zhè shuāng zěnmeyàng?

Lǐ xiǎojie: Yě bù xíng, zhè shuāng <u>gēn</u> nà shuāng <u>yíyàng</u> (G6) dà.

Shòuhuòyuán: Nà zhè shuāng hēi de ne?

Lǐ xiǎojie: Zhè shuāng xié <u>suīrán</u> dàxiǎo héshì, <u>kěshì</u> (G7) yánsè bù
                    hǎo. Yǒu méiyǒu kāfēisè de?

Shòuhuòyuán: Duìbuqǐ, zhǐ yǒu hēi de.

Lǐ xiǎojie: Nà hǎo ba. Wǒ hái yào fù qián ma?

Shòuhuòyuán: Bú yòng, zhè shuāng de qián gēn nà shuāng yíyàng.

Dialogue II: *Chinese*

李小姐：對不起，這雙鞋太小了。能不能換一
　　　　雙？

售貨員：沒問題。您看，這雙怎麼樣？

李小姐：也不行，這雙跟那雙一樣 (G6) 大。

售貨員：那這雙黑的呢？

李小姐：這雙鞋雖然大小合適，可是 (G7) 顏色不
　　　　好。有沒有咖啡色的？

售貨員：對不起，只有黑的。

李小姐：那好吧。我還要付錢嗎？

售貨員：不用，這雙的錢跟那雙一樣。

Supplementary Vocabulary

1.	賣	mài	V	to sell
2.	裙子	qúnzi	N	skirt
3.	大衣	dàyī	N	overcoat
4.	夾克	jiákè	N	jacket
5.	外套	wàitào	N	coat; jacket
6.	西裝	xīzhuāng	N	suit
7.	毛衣	máoyī	N	sweater
8.	T-恤衫	T-xùshān	N	T-shirt
9.	戴	dài	V	to wear (hat, glasses, etc.)
10.	帽子	màozi	N	hat
11.	頂	dǐng	M	(a measure word for hat)
12.	襪子	wàzi	N	socks
13.	長	cháng	Adj	long
14.	短	duǎn	Adj	short
15.	藍	lán	Adj	blue
16.	綠	lǜ	Adj	green
17.	紫	zǐ	Adj	purple
18.	粉紅色	fěnhóngsè	Adj	pink
19.	橘紅色	júhóngsè	Adj	orange
20.	灰	huī	Adj	grey

GRAMMAR

1. The Auxiliary Verb 要 (yào) (II) [See also L.6 G2]

One of the meanings of 要 (yào) is "to have the volition to do something." For instance,

(1) 明天是週末，你要做什麼？

  Míngtiān shì zhōumò, nǐ yào zuò shénme?

  (Tomorrow is the weekend. What do you want to do?)

(2) 我要去圖書館看書，你去不去？

  Wǒ yào qù túshūguǎn kàn shū, nǐ qù bu qù?

  (I want to go to the library to read. Are you going?)

(3) 我要喝可樂，他要喝啤酒。

  Wǒ yào hē kělè, tā yào hē píjiǔ.

  (I would like to have a cola, and he wants a beer.)

To negate, use 不想(bù xiǎng). For instance,

(4) 我不想去圖書館。

  Wǒ bù xiǎng qù túshūguǎn.

  (I don't feel like going to the library.)

(5) 今天我不想做功課。

  Jīntiān wǒ bù xiǎng zuò gōngkè.

  (I don't feel like doing my homework.)

Some Chinese, particularly in the south, however, would say, "我不要去圖書館(Wǒ búyào qù túshūguǎn)" for (4).

Note: Both modal verbs 想 (xiǎng) and 要 (yào) can express a desire or an intention, but 要 (yào) carries a stronger tone.

2. Measure Words (II) [See also L.2 G1]

The following are the "measure word + noun" combinations that we have covered so far.

一杯茶	yì bēi chá	a cup of tea
一封信	yì fēng xìn	a letter
一個人	yí ge rén	a person
一節課	yì jié kè	a class
一件襯衫	yí jiàn chènshān	a shirt
一篇日記	yì piān rìjì	a diary
一瓶啤酒	yì píng píjiǔ	a bottle of beer
一雙鞋	yì shuāng xié	a pair of shoes
一條褲子	yì tiáo kùzi	a pair of pants
一位先生	yí wèi xiānsheng	a gentleman
一張照片	yì zhāng zhàopiàn	a picture

Supplementary:

一本書	yì běn shū	a book
一張紙	yì zhāng zhǐ	a piece of paper
一枝筆	yì zhī bǐ	a pen
一隻鞋	yì zhī xié	a shoe [See also "a pair of shoes" above]

3. 的 (de) Structure

We have a 的 (de) structure when a noun, a pronoun, or an adjective is followed by the structural particle 的 (de). Grammatically, a 的 (de) structure is equivalent to a noun, e.g., 老師的 (lǎoshī de, the teacher's), 我的 (wǒ de, mine), 大的 (dà de, the big one), etc.

4. 多 (duō) Used Interrogatively

(1) 你今年多大？ (See Lesson 3)

Nǐ jīnnián duō dà?

(How old are you this year?)

(2) **你穿多大的衣服？**

　　Nǐ chuān duō dà de yīfu?

　　(What size clothes do you wear?)

(3) **你弟弟多高？**

　　Nǐ dìdi duō gāo?

　　(How tall is your younger brother?)

5. Amounts of Money

Chinese monetary units are 元 (yuán, Yuan or a Chinese dollar)，角 (jiǎo, dime or 1/10 of a Yuan)，and 分 (fēn, cent or 1/100 of a Yuan)，which are referred to in colloquial Chinese as 塊 (kuài)，毛 (máo)，分 (fēn) respectively. It is permitted to use abbreviated forms when talking about money. The rules for omissions are as follows: You must begin by omitting the last word 錢 in the expression, and then the second to the last. For example, for the expression 五塊九毛九分錢 (wǔ kuài jiǔ máo jiǔ fēn qián, $5.99), you can say 五塊九毛九分 (wǔ kuài jiǔ máo jiǔ fēn) without the 錢 (qián) or 五塊九毛九 (wǔ kuài jiǔ máo jiǔ) without the 錢 (qián) and the 分 (fēn). However, you cannot say *五塊九毛九錢 (*wǔ kuài jiǔ máo jiǔ qián) by omitting the 分 (fēn) without first omitting the 錢 (qián). Sometimes the word 分 (fēn)，and also the word 角 (jiǎo), if the number for 分 happens to be zero, can be omitted in colloquial expressions. All zeroes between two non-zero numerals should be connected by a 零 (líng, zero), e.g.:

(1) $8. 55　　**八塊五毛五 (分)(錢)**　　bā kuài wǔ máo wǔ (fēn)(qián)

(2) $15. 30　　**十五塊三 (毛) (錢)**　　shíwǔ kuài sān (máo) (qián)

(3) $103　　　**一百零三塊 (錢)**　　yì bǎi líng sān kuài (qián)

(4) $100. 30　**一百塊零三毛 (錢)**　　yì bǎi kuài líng sān máo (qián)

(5) $100. 03　**一百塊零三分 (錢)**　　yìbǎi kuài líng sān fēn (qián)

Note: To avoid ambiguity, 毛 (máo) and 分 (fēn) cannot be omitted in sentences (4) and (5) above.

6. <u>跟／和...（不）一樣</u> (gēn/hé... {bù} yíyàng, {not the} same as...)

　　To express similarity or dissimilarity as the result of a comparison, the structure 跟／和...（不）一樣 (gēn/hé... {bù} yíyàng) is used.

(1) 你的襯衫跟我的一樣。

Nǐ de chènshān gēn wǒ de yíyàng.

(Your shirt is the same as mine.)

(2) 貴的衣服和便宜的衣服不一樣。

Guì de yīfu hé piányi de yīfu bù yíyàng.

(Expensive clothes are different from cheap ones.)

Following 一樣 (yíyàng) an adjective can be used:

(3) 弟弟跟哥哥一樣高。

Dìdi gēn gēge yíyàng gāo.

(The younger brother is as tall as the older one.)

7. 雖然..., 可是/但是... (suīrán..., kěshì/dànshì..., although...yet...)

This pair of conjunctions are used respectively in the two clauses of a complex sentence, but sometimes 雖然 (suīrán) is omitted.

(1) 雖然這雙鞋很便宜，可是大小不合適。

Suīrán zhè shuāng xié hěn piányi, kěshì dàxiǎo bù héshì.

(Although this pair of shoes is not expensive, it's not my size.)

(2) 這本書很有意思，可是太貴了。

Zhè běn shū hěn yǒu yìsi, kěshì tài guì le.

(This book is very interesting, but it's too expensive.)

(3) 中文不容易，但是很有意思。

Zhōngwén bù róngyì, dànshì hěn yǒuyìsi.

(Chinese is not easy, but it is very interesting.)

But if 雖然 (suīrán) is used in the first clause, 可是 (kěshì) cannot be omitted in the second clause. The following sentence is therefore incorrect.

(2a) **Incorrect:** 雖然這本書很有意思，太貴了。

Suīrán zhè běn shū hěn yǒu yìsi, tài guì le.

PATTERN DRILLS

A. 要 (yào, to want to; to have a desire for)

1. Tā de péngyou	yào	mǎi yì tiáo hóng qúnzi.
2. Lǐ Yǒu		chuān kāfēisè de yīfu qù tiào wǔ.
3. Dìdi zhège zhōumò		kàn wàiguó diànyǐng.
4. Jiějie xǐle zǎo yǐhòu		qù túshūguǎn kàn shū.
5. Wǒ xué Zhōngwén de shíhou		yòng diànnǎo liànxí fāyīn.
6. Wǒ mèimei xīngqītiān		qù tóngxué jiā wánr.
7. Nǐ gēge		mǎi shénme yīfu?

1. 她的朋友	要	買一條紅裙子。
2. 李友		穿咖啡色的衣服去跳舞。
3. 弟弟這個週末		看外國電影。
4. 姐姐洗了澡以後		去圖書館看書。
5. 我學中文的時候		用電腦練習發音。
6. 我妹妹星期天		去同學家玩兒。
7. 你哥哥		買什麼衣服？

B. 想 (xiǎng, to want to; to feel like; would like to)

1. Tā	xiǎng	xué Zhōngwén.
2. Wǒ		kàn Zhōngguó diànyǐng.
3. Wǒ wǎnshang		yùxí shēngcí.
4. Xiǎo Gāo		qǐng péngyou chī fàn.
5. Lǐ Yǒu wǎnfàn yǐhòu		qù Xiǎo Gāo jiā kàn diànshì.
6. Wáng Péng jīntiān bù		qù kàn diànyǐng.
7. Zhè jiàn yīfu wǒ bù		mǎi.
8. Míngtiān yǒu kǎoshì, Xiǎo Lín		gēn péngyou fùxí yǔfǎ.

1. 他	想	學中文。
2. 我		看中國電影。

3. 我晚上　　　　　　想　　　　　預習生詞。

4. 小高　　　　　　　　　　　　請朋友吃飯。

5. 李友晚飯以後　　　　　　去小高家看電視。

6. 王朋今天不　　　　　　　去看電影。

7. 這件衣服我不　　　　　　買。

8. 明天有考試，小林　　　　跟朋友復習語法。

C. 的 (de) Structure

1. Zhè jiàn yīfu shì wǒ de.
2. Nà běn shū shì lǎoshī de.
3. Zhè tiáo qúnzi hé zhè jiàn yīfu dōu shì mèimei de.
4. Xié tā yào mǎi qī hào de.
5. Kùzi tā xǐhuan chuān kāfēisè de.

1. 這件衣服是我的。

2. 那本書是老師的。

3. 這條裙子和這件衣服都是妹妹的。

4. 鞋她要買七號的。

5. 褲子他喜歡穿咖啡色的。

D. 多 (duō)

1. Nǐ de dìdi jīnnián　　duō　　dà?
2. Tā de kùzi　　　　　　　　guì?
3. Tā chuān de yīfu　　　　　dà?
4. Nǐ de péngyou　　　　　　gāo?
5. Nà jiàn chènshān　　　　　guì?

1. 你的弟弟今年　　多　　大？

2. 他的褲子　　　　　　貴？

3. 她穿的衣服　　　　　大？

4. 你的朋友   高？

5. 那件襯衫   貴？

E. 跟...一樣 (gēn...yíyàng; the same as...)

1. Zhè jiàn yifu	gēn	nà jiàn	yíyàng	piàoliang.
2. Tā		wǒ gēge		gāo.
3. Měiguófàn		Zhōngguófàn		hǎochī.
4. Tā de chènshān		wǒ de		guì.
5. Zhōngwén		Rìwén		nán.
6. Zhè shuāng xié		nà shuāng		héshì.
7. Jīntiān de shēngcí		zuótiān de		duō.
8. Zhège xuéxiào		nàge		hǎo.

1. 這件衣服   跟 [gen]   那件   一樣   漂亮。

2. 他   我哥哥   高。

3. 美國飯   中國飯   好吃。

4. 他的襯衫   我的   貴。

5. 中文   日文   難。

6. 這雙鞋   那雙   合適。

7. 今天的生詞   昨天的   多。

8. 這個學校   那個   好。

F. 雖然...可是/但是 (suīrán...kěshì/dànshì; although...but)

1. Suīrán	Zhōngwén hěn nán,	kěshì	wǒ juéde hěn yǒu yìsi.
2.	tā de yifu hěn duō,		méiyǒu héshì de.
3.	dì-bā kè de yǔfǎ hěn nán,		wǒ dōu dǒng le.
4.	jīntiān de gōngkè hěn duō,		tā dōu zuò le.
5.	zhè jiàn yifu de yánsè hěn hǎokàn,		tài xiǎo le.
6.	wǎnshang de diànshì hěn búcuò,		wǒ méiyǒu shíjiān kàn.
7.	Lǐ Yǒu hěn xǐhuan tiàowǔ,		tā jīntiān méiyǒu kòngr.

1. **雖然** 中文很難， **可是** 我覺得很有意思。

2. 她的衣服很多， 沒有合適的。

3. 第八課的語法很難， 我都懂了。

4. 今天的功課很多， 他都做了。

5. 這件衣服的顏色不錯， 太小了。

6. 晚上的電視很不錯， 我沒有時間看。

7. 李友很喜歡跳舞， 她今天沒有空兒。

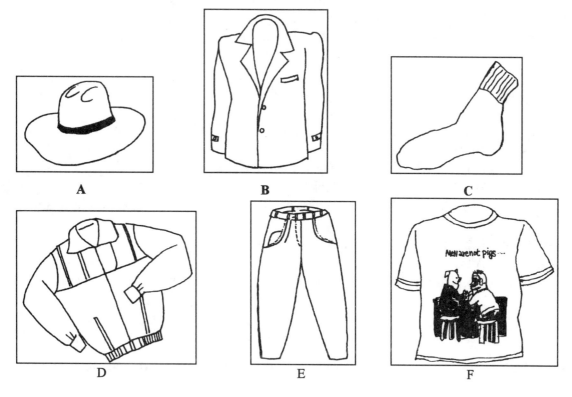

Do you know how to say the clothing items above?

Don't forget to use the appropriate measure words!

ENGLISH TEXT

Dialogue I

(Shopping for clothes)

Salesperson: Miss, what are you looking for?

Miss Li: I'd like to buy a shirt.

Salesperson: What color do you like? Yellow or red?

Miss Li: I like red. I'd also like to get a pair of pants.

Salesperon: What size? Large, medium or small?

Miss Li: Medium. Something not too expensive, but not too cheap, either.

Salesperson: How about these pants and this shirt?

Miss Li: Great. Where do I pay?

Salesperson: Here.

Miss Li: How much altogether?

Salesperson: Twenty dollars and fifty cents for the shirt, and thirty-two ninety-nine for the pants. Fifty-three dollars forty-nine cents altogether.

Miss Li: OK. Here is one hundred.

Salesperson: Forty-six fifty-one is your change. Thank you.

Dialogue II

Miss Li: Excuse me, this pair of shoes is too small. Can I exchange them?

Salesperson: No problem. How about this pair?

Miss Li: No, that won't do. This pair is the same size as the other pair.

Salesperson: What about this pair in black?

Miss Li: Although this pair is the right size, it's not a good color. Do you have any in brown?

Salesperson: I'm sorry. We've only got black ones left.

Miss Li: All right then. Do I have to pay?

Salesperson: No, that won't be necessary. This pair is the same price as the other one.

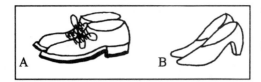

Which pair of the shoes in the picture is mentioned in Dialogue II of this lesson? Why?

Lesson Ten   Talking about the Weather
第十課   談天氣

DIALOGUE I: *THE WEATHER IS GETTING BETTER*

Vocabulary

1.	天氣	tiānqì	N	weather
2.	比	bǐ	Prep.	(indicates comparison) [See G1]
3.	下雨	xià yǔ	VO	to rain
4.	報上	bàoshang		in/on the newspaper
5.	預報	yùbào	N	forecast
6.	更	gèng	Adv	even more (used in comparison)

7.	不但...而且	búdàn..., érqiě	Conj	not only..., but also
8.	會	huì	AV	(indicates probability) [See G3]
9.	暖和	nuǎnhuo	Adj	warm (weather)
10.	一點兒	yìdiǎnr		a bit
11.	約	yuē	V	to make an appointment with (someone)
12.	公園	gōngyuán	N	park
13.	紅葉	hóngyè	N	red autumn leaves
14.	怎麼辦	zěnme bàn	QW	what to do
15.	錄像	lùxiàng	N	video recording

Proper Nouns

16.	謝	xiè		(a surname); thanks
17.	上海	Shànghǎi		Shanghai (name of a city in China)
	海	hǎi	N	sea; ocean

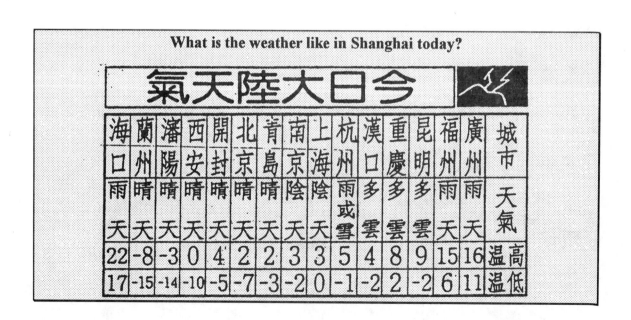

What is the weather like in Shanghai today?

Dialogue I: *Pinyin*

Xiè xiǎojie:	Jīntiān tiānqì bǐ [G1] zuótiān hǎo, bú xiàyǔ le [G2].
Gāo xiānsheng:	Míngtiān tiānqì zěnmeyàng? Xīwàng míngtiān yě bú xiàyǔ.
Xiè xiǎojie:	Wǒ kànle bàoshang de tiānqì yùbào, míngtiān tiānqì bǐ jīntiān gèng hǎo. Búdàn bú huì [G3] xiàyǔ, érqiě huì nuǎnhuo yìdiǎnr.
Gāo xiānsheng:	Tài hǎo le! Wǒ yuēle Lǐ xiǎojie míngtiān qù gōngyuán kàn hóngyè.
Xiè xiǎojie:	Shì ma? Kěshì Lǐ xiǎojie jīntiān zǎoshang gēn Wáng xiānsheng qù Shànghǎi le.
Gāo xiānsheng	Zhēn de a? Nà wǒ míngtiān zěnme bàn?
Xiè xiǎojie:	Nǐ zài jiā kàn lùxiàng ba!

Do the pictures above accurately depict Dialogue I?
Please explain each picture separately.

Dialogue I: *Chinese*

謝小姐：今天天氣比^(G1)昨天好，不下雨了^(G2)。

高先生：明天天氣怎麼樣？希望明天也不下雨。

謝小姐：我看了報上的天氣預報，明天天氣比今
天更好。不但不會^(G3)下雨，而且會暖和
一點兒。

高先生：太好了！我約了李小姐明天去公園看紅
葉。

謝小姐：是嗎？可是李小姐今天早上跟王先生
去上海了。

高先生：真的啊？那我明天怎麼辦？

謝小姐：你在家看錄像吧！

DIALOGUE II: *COMPLAINING ABOUT THE WEATHER*

Vocabulary

1. 糟糕	zāogāo	Adj	in a terrible mess; too bad; bad luck
2. 又	yòu	Adv	again
3. 剛才	gāngcái	T	just now; a short moment ago
4. 這個	zhège	Pr	this
5. 出去	chūqu	VP	to go out

6. 熱	rè	Adj	hot
7. 舒服	shūfu	Adj	comfortable
8. 夏天	xiàtiān	N	summer
9. 這樣	zhèyàng	Pr	so; like this
10. 涼快	liángkuai	Adj	nice and cool (weather)
11. 春天	chūntiān	N	spring
12. 冬天	dōngtiān	N	winter
13. 又...又...	yòu...yòu		both...and...
14. 冷	lěng	Adj	cold
15. 悶	mēn	Adj	stuffy
16. 下次	xià cì		next time
次	cì	M	time; (a measure word for occurrence)
17. 最好	zuìhǎo	Adv	had better
18. 秋天	qiūtiān	N	autumn; fall

Proper Nouns

20. 台北	Táiběi	N	Taipei (name of a city in Taiwan)
21. 台灣	Táiwān	N	Taiwan

   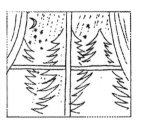

Dialogue II

Xiǎo Yè: Zhēn zāogāo, yòu ^(G4) xià dà yǔ le.

Xiǎo Xià: Gāngcái wǒ kàn bào le, bàoshang shuō, zhège xīngqī tiānqì

              dōu bù hǎo, xià ge xīngqī tiānqì cái huì ^(G3) hǎo.

Xiǎo Yè: Zhēn de a? Nà zhège zhōumò bù néng chūqu wán le. Zuìjìn

              tiānqì tài rè, zhēn bù shūfu.

Xiǎo Xià   Táiběi xiàtiān de tiānqì jiù shi zhèyàng. Liǎng ge yuè yǐhòu, tiānqì

              jiù huì bǐ xiànzài liángkuai yìdiǎnr le.

Xiǎo Yè: Liǎng ge yuè yǐhòu? Xiàge yuè, wǒ jiù huí Měiguó qu le.

Xiǎo Xià   Táiwān chūntiān chángcháng xiàyǔ, dōngtiān hěn lěng, xiàtiān

              yòu mēn yòu rè ^(G5). Nǐ xià cì zuìhǎo qiūtiān lái.

Dialogue II

小葉：真糟糕，<u>又</u>(G4)下大雨了。

小夏：剛才我看報了，報上說，這個星期天氣都不好，下個星期天氣才<u>會</u>(G3)好。

小葉：真的啊？那這個週末不能出去玩了。最近天氣太熱，真不舒服。

小夏：台北夏天的天氣就是這樣。兩個月以後，天氣就會比現在涼快一點兒了。

小葉：兩個月以後？下個月我就回美國去了。

小夏：台灣春天常常下雨，冬天很冷，夏天<u>又悶又熱</u>(G5)。你下次最好秋天來。

Supplementary Vocabulary

1.	潮濕	cháoshī	Adj	wet; humid
2.	雲	yún	N	cloud
3.	雪	xuě	N	snow
4.	晴	qíng	Adj	sunny; clear
5.	陰	yīn	Adj	overcast
6.	台中	Táizhōng	N	Taichung (name of a city in Taiwan)
7.	加拿大	Jiānádà	N	Canada
8.	溫哥華	Wēngēhuá	N	Vancouver
9.	香港	Xiānggǎng	N	Hong Kong

GRAMMAR

1. Comparative Sentences with 比 (bǐ)

A comparison is usually expressed by using the structural marker 比 (bǐ) in the basic pattern: A 比 (bǐ) B + Adj., e.g.:

(1) 李友比她姐姐高。

　　　Lǐ Yǒu bǐ tā jiějie gāo.

　　　(Li You is taller than her older sister.)

(2) 今天比昨天冷。

　　　Jīntiān bǐ zuótiān lěng.

　　　(It is colder today than yesterday.)

(3) 這本書比那本書有意思。

　　　Zhè běn shū bǐ nà běn shū yǒu yìsi.

　　　(This book is more interesting than that one.)

Note: In a comparative sentence, if an intensifier or other modifier of the adjective has to be used, it cannot be put before the adjective but only after it, as in (4) and (5) below. Possible exceptions to this rule are a few monosyllabic adverbs such as 更 in (6).

(4) 今天比昨天冷一點兒。

　　　Jīntiān bǐ zuótiān lěng yì diǎnr.

　　　(It is a bit colder today than yesterday.)

(5) 明天會比今天冷得多。

　　　Míngtiān huì bǐ jīntiān lěng de duō.

　　　(It will be much colder tomorrow than today.)

(6) 昨天冷，今天比昨天更冷。

　　　Zuótiān lěng, jīntiān bǐ zuótiān gèng lěng.

　　　(It was cold yesterday. Today is even colder than yesterday.)

(7) 今天比昨天冷多了。

　　　Jīntiān bǐ zuótiān lěng duō le.

　　　(Today is much colder than yesterday.)

The following sentences are incorrect:

(7a) **Incorrect:** 今天比昨天很冷。

Jīntiān bǐ zuótiān hěn lěng.

(8a) **Incorrect:** 今天比昨天一點冷。

Jīntiān bǐ zuótiān yì diǎnr lěng.

2. 了 (le) (III) [See also L.5 G5 and L.8 G6]: 了 as Sentence-Final Particle

When 了 (le) occurs at the end of a sentence, it often indicates a change of status or the realization of a new situation, e.g.:

(1) 下雨了。

Xià yǔ le.

(It's raining now.)

(2) 妹妹的衣服小了。

Mèimei de yīfu xiǎo le.

(My sister's clothes have become too small for her.)

(3) 我昨天沒有空兒，今天有空兒了。

Wǒ zuótiān méiyǒu kòngr, jīntiān yǒu kòng le.

(I didn't have time yesterday, but I do today.)

(4) 你看，老師來了。

Nǐ kàn, lǎoshī lái le.

(Look, the teacher has come.)

When used in this sense, 了 can still be used at the end of a sentence even if the sentence is in the negative.

(5) 我沒有錢了，不買了。

Wǒ méiyǒu qián le, bù mǎi le.

(I no longer have any money. I won't buy it anymore.) [Indicating that I intended to buy it originally, but I have changed my mind.]

Note: To negate 有 (yǒu, to have), use 沒 (méi), not 不 (bù).

3. The Auxiliary Verb 會 (huì) (II) [See also L.8 G9]

會 (huì) indicates an anticipated event or action in the future.

(1) 白老師現在不在辦公室，可是他明天會在。

Bái lǎoshī xiànzài bú zài bāngōngshì, kěshì tā míngtiān huì zài.

(Teacher Bai is not in the office now, but he will be there tomorrow.)

(2) A：你明年做什麼？

Nǐ míngnián zuò shénme?

(What will you do next year?)

B：我明年會去中國學中文。

Wǒ míngnián huì qù Zhōngguó xué Zhōngwén.

(I will go to China to learn Chinese next year.)

(3) 他說他晚上會給你打電話。

Tā shuō tā wǎnshang huì gěi nǐ dǎ diànhuà.

(He said he will call you this evening.)

The negative form for 會 (huì) is 不會 (bú huì)：

(4) 小王覺得不舒服，今天不會來上課。

Xiǎo Wáng juéde bù shūfu, jīntiān bú huì lái shàngkè.

(Xiao Wang is not feeling well. She won't come to class today.)

(5) 她很忙，晚上不會去看電影。

Tā hěn máng, wǎnshang bú huì qù kàn diànyǐng.

(She is too busy and is not going to see the movie tonight.)

4. The Adverb 又 (yòu, again)

又 (yòu, again) indicates repetition of an action, e.g.:

(1) 我昨天看電影了，今天又看電影了。

Wǒ zuótiān kàn diànyǐng le, jīntiān yòu kàn diànyǐng le.

(I saw a movie yesterday, and I saw another one today.)

(2) 前天下 轇 昨天又下雨了。

Qiántiān xiàyǔ, zuótiān yòu xià yǔ le.

(It rained the day before yesterday, and yesterday it rained again.)

(3) 媽媽昨天又給我打電話了。

Māma zuótiān yòu gěi wǒ dǎ diànhuà le.

(My mom called me again yesterday.)

Note: Both 又 (yòu, again) and 再 (zài, again) can indicate repetition of an action, but in a sentence with 又 (yòu, again), both the original action and the repetition usually occurred in the past, while 再 (zài, again) denotes an anticipated repetition of an action.

(4) 我上個週末跳舞了，昨天我又去跳舞了。

Wǒ shàngge zhōumo tiào wǔ le, zuótiān wǒ yòu qù tiào wǔ le.

(I danced last weekend. Yesterday I went dancing again.)

(5) 我昨天跳舞了，我想明天晚上再去跳舞。

Wǒ zuótiān tiào wǔ le, wǒ xiǎng míngtiān wǎnshang zài qù tiào wǔ.

(I danced yesterday. I'm thinking of going dancing again tomorrow night.)

5. <u>又. . . 又. . .</u> (yòu...yòu..., both...and...)

The two adjectives used in this structure are either both commendatory or both derogatory, e.g., 又悶又熱 (yòu mēn yòu rè, both stuffy and humid)[both adjectives or qualities are perceived to be derogatory] , 又便宜又好 (yòu piányi yòu hǎo, both inexpensive and good) [both adjectives are commendatory].

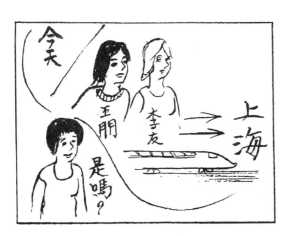

Does this scene look familiar?

Where have you seen it?

Try to locate the sentence depicting it in this lesson.

PATTERN DRILLS

A. Comparative Sentences with 比 (bǐ)

1. Yīngwén	bǐ	Zhōngwén	róngyì.
2. Dì liù kè		dì wǔ kè	nán.
3. Tiàowǔ		tīng yīnyuè	yǒuyìsi.
4. Lǐ xiǎojie		Wáng xiānsheng	máng.
5. Tā gēge		tā dìdi	gāo.
6. Tā dìdi		tā gēge	shuài.
7. Zhè jiàn yīfu		nà jiàn yīfu	piányi.
8. Nà běn shū		zhè běn shū	guì.
9. Tā de qián		wǒ de qián	duō.
10. Jīntiān de tiānqì		zuótiān de tiānqì	nuǎnhuo.
11. Shànghǎi		Táiběi	lěng.

1. 英文	比	中文	容易。
2. 第六課		第五課	難。
3. 跳舞		聽音樂	有意思。
4. 李小姐		王先生	忙。
5. 她哥哥		她弟弟	高。
6. 他弟弟		他哥哥	帥。
7. 這件衣服		那件衣服	便宜。
8. 那本書		這本書	貴。
9. 她的錢		我的錢	多。
10. 今天的天氣		昨天的天氣	暖和。
11. 上海		台北	冷。

B. Sentential-Final Particle 了 (le)

Example: Zuótiān xiàyǔ le. (jīntiān, bú xià yǔ)
     ---> Jīntiān bú xià yǔ le.

昨天下雨。（今天，不下雨）

--> 今天不下雨了。

1. Wǒ qùnián xué Yīngwén. (jīnnián xué Zhōngwén)
2. Tā zǎoshang xǐ zǎo le. (wǎnshang bù xǐ zǎo)
3. Wǒ zuótiān chī Zhōngguófàn le. (jīntiān bù chī Zhōngguófàn)
4. Lǐ Yǒu yǐqián xǐhuan chàng gē. (xiànzài xǐhuan tiào wǔ)
5. Tā yǐqián xǐhuan Zhōngguó yīnyuè. (xiànzài xǐhuān Měiguó yīnyuè)
6. Wǒ yǐqián bú huì yòng Zhōngwén (xiànzài huì yòng Zhōngwén
   xiě xìn. xiě xìn)
7. Wǒ mèimei yǐqián chuān báisè de xié (xiànzài chuān hēisè de xié)
8. Shàngge xīngqī zhèr hěn rè. (xiànzài liángkuai)

1. 我去年學英文。 （今年 學中文）

2. 他早上洗澡了。 （晚上 不洗澡）

3. 我昨天吃中國飯了。 （今天 不吃中國飯）

4. 李友以前喜歡唱歌。 （現在 喜歡跳舞）

5. 他以前喜歡中國音樂。 （現在 喜歡美國音樂）

6. 我以前不會用中文寫信。 （現在 會用中文寫信）

7. 我妹妹以前穿白色的鞋。 （現在 穿黑色的鞋）

8. 上個星期這兒很熱。 （現在 涼快）

C. 不但...而且 (búdàn...érqiě)

C1:
1. <u>Tā búdàn</u> huì shuō Zhōngwén, <u>érqiě</u> huì shuō Yīnwén.
2. xǐhuan chàng gē, xǐhuan tiào wǔ.
3. huì zuò Měiguó fàn huì zuò Zhōngguófàn.
4. kàn diànyǐng kàn diànshì.
5. xǐhuan bái yánsè xǐhuan hóng yánsè.
6. liànxí le fāyīn tīng le kèwén lùyīn.
7. fùxí le dì qī kè yùxí le dì bā kè.

C1:

1. 他 <u>不但</u> 會說中文，   <u>而且</u>   會說英文。
2.   喜歡唱歌，   喜歡跳舞。
3.   會做美國飯   會做中國飯。
4.   看電影   看電視。
5.   喜歡白顏色   喜歡紅顏色。
6.   練習了發音   聽了課文錄音。
7.   復習了第七課   預習了第八課。

C2:

1. Tāde dìdi   <u>búdàn</u>   hěn gāo, <u>érqiě</u>   hěn shuài.
2. Zhè jiàn yīfu   tài dà,   yánsè bùhǎo.
3. Jīntiān de tiānqì   mēn,   rè.
4. Táiwān de dōngtiān   lěng,   cháoshī.
5. Dì shí kè de shēngcí   duō,   nán.
6. Zhè shuāng xié   guì,   bù shūfu.
7. Tā xiězì   hǎo,   kuài.
8. Xiǎo Gāo de jiā   hěn dà,   hěn piàoliang.

C2:

1. 他的弟弟   <u>不但</u>   很高，<u>而且</u>   很帥。
2. 這件衣服   太大，   顏色不好。
3. 今天的天氣   悶   熱。
4. 台灣的冬天   冷   潮濕。
5. 第十課的生詞   多   難。
6. 這雙鞋   貴   不舒服。
7. 他寫字   好   快。
8. 小高的家   很大   很漂亮。

D. 會 (huì)

Example: Míngtiān xià yǔ.
    ---> Míngtiān huì xià yǔ.
    ---> Míngtiān bú huì xià yǔ.

明天 下雨

--> 明天會下雨。

--> 明天不會下雨。

1. Xiǎo Wáng	míngnián	qù Táiwān.
2. Wáng Péng	jīntiān wǎnshang	jiāo Lǐ Yǒu xiě zì.
3. Wǒmen	zhōumò	liànxí Zhōngwén.
4. Lǐ lǎoshī	xiàwǔ	qù kāi huì.
5. Wáng lǎoshī	míngtiān	qù kàn hóngyè.
6. Xiǎo Gāo	xīngqīliù	qù tiào wǔ.
7. Xiǎo Bái	xīngqītiān	qǐng wǒmen chī fàn.
8. Lǐ Xiǎojie	míngtiān xiàwǔ	qù mǎi yīfu.

1. 小王	明年	去台灣。
2. 王朋	今天晚上	教李友寫字。
3. 我們	週末	練習中文。
4. 李老師	下午	去開會。
5. 王老師	明天	去看紅葉。
6. 小高	星期六	去跳舞。
7. 小白	星期天	請我們吃飯。
8. 李小姐	明天下午	去買衣服。

E. 又 (yòu)

Example: Wǒ zuótiān kànle yí ge diànyǐng, jīntiān yòu kànle yí ge diànyǐng.
    (xīngqīyī/xīngqī'èr   yòu   Zhōngwénkè)
    ---> Wǒ xīngqīyī yǒu Zhōngwénkè, xīngqī'èr yòu yǒu Zhōngwénkè.

我昨天看了一個電影，今天又看了一個電影。

（星期一／星期二 有 中文課）

--> 我星期一有中文課，星期二又有中文課。

1. zuótián shàngwǔ/jīntián xiàwǔ	dǎle yí ge diànhuà
2. zuótiān/jīntiān	mǎile yí jiàn yīfu
3. shàng kè yǐqián/xià kè yǐhòu	tīngle yí cì lùyīn
4. qùnián/jīnnián chūntiān	qùle yí cì Táiwān
5. zuótiān/jīntiān	qù kàn hóngyè le
6. zuótiān wǎnshang/jīntiān wǎnshang	tiào wǔ le
7. shàngge xīngqī/zhège xīngqī	kàn le yí ge Rìběn diànyǐng

1. 昨天上午／今天下午　　　　　打了一個電話

2. 昨天／今天　　　　　　　　　買了一件衣服

3. 上課以前／下課以後　　　　　聽了一次錄音

4. 去年／今年春天　　　　　　　去了一次台灣

5. 昨天／今天　　　　　　　　　去看紅葉了

6. 昨天晚上／今天晚上　　　　　跳舞了

7. 上個星期／這個星期　　　　　看了一個日本電影

F. <u>又...又...</u> (yòu...yòu..., both...and...)

1. Zhè shuāng xié	<u>yòu</u>	piányi	<u>yòu</u>	hǎokàn.
2. Zhè jiàn yīfu		guì		nánkàn.
3. Zhège diànnǎo		hǎo		piányi.
4. Shànghǎi de xiàtiān		rè		mēn.
5. Táiwān de dōngtiān		lěng		cháoshī.
6. Tā de dìdi		gāo		shuài.
7. Zhè běn shū		guì		méi yìsi.
8. Dì-bā kè		róngyì		yǒu yìsi.
9. Xiǎo Gāo de jiā		shūfu		piàoliang.

1. 這雙鞋　　　　又　　　　便宜　　　又　　　好看。
2. 這件衣服　　　　　　　貴　　　　　　　難看。
3. 這個電腦　　　　　　　好　　　　　　　便宜。
4. 上海的夏天　　　　　　熱　　　　　　　悶。
5. 台灣的冬天　　　　　　冷　　　　　　　潮濕。
6. 他的弟弟　　　　　　　高　　　　　　　帥。
7. 這本書　　　　　　　　貴　　　　　　　沒意思。
8. 第八課　　　　　　　　容易　　　　　　有意思。
9. 小高的家　　　　　　　舒服　　　　　　漂亮。

**Review Dialogue I of this lesson and put the four pictures
above in the correct order by using numbers 1-4.**

ENGLISH TEXT

Dialogue I

Miss Xie:	The weather is better today than yesterday. It's no longer raining.
Mr. Lan:	What's the weather going to be like tomorrow? I hope it won't rain tomorrow, either.
Miss Xie:	I read the weather forecast in today's paper. The weather will be even better tomorrow than today. It not only won't rain, it will also be a bit warmer.
Mr. Lan:	That's great. I asked Miss Li to go to the park with me to see the red leaves tomorrow.
Miss Xie:	Really? But Miss Li went to Shanghai this morning with Mr. Wang.
Mr. Lan:	You don't say! What shall I do tomorrow?
Miss Xie:	You can watch a video at home!

Dialogue II

Xiao Ye:	Too bad. It's pouring again.
Xiao Xia:	I just read the newspaper. The paper says the weather is going to be bad all this week. It will be next week before the weather gets better.
Xiao Ye:	Really? Then we can't go out this weekend. It's been too hot lately. It's really uncomfortable.
Xiao Xia:	The weather is like this in the summer in Taipei. In two months the weather will be a bit cooler than it is now.
Xiao Ye:	In two months? I'm going back to the United States next month.
Xiao Xia:	In Taiwan, it rains often in spring, and it's cold in winter. In summer it's hot and muggy. Next time you'd best come in the fall.

Lesson Eleven   Transportation
第十一課   交通

DIALOGUE: *GOING HOME FOR THE WINTER VACATION*

Vocabulary

1. 寒假	hánjià	N	winter vacation
2. 飛機	fēijī	N	airplane
飛	fēi	V	to fly
機	jī	N	machine
3. 票	piào	N	ticket
4. (飛)機場	(fēi)jīchǎng	N	airport
5. 坐	zuò	V	to travel by [See also L.5]

6. 公共汽車	gōnggòng qìchē		bus
公共	gōnggòng	Adj	public
汽車	qìchē	N	automobile
車	chē	N	vehicle; car
7. 或者	huòzhě	Conj	or [See G2]
8. 地鐵	dìtiě	N	subway
9. 走	zǒu	V	to walk; to go by way of
10. 先	xiān	Adv	first; before
11. (車)站	(chē)zhàn	N	(of bus, train, etc.) stop; station
12. 下車	xià chē	VO	to get off (a bus, train, etc.)
13. 然後	ránhòu	Adv	then
14. 綠	lǜ	Adj	green
15. 線	xiàn	N	line
16. 最後	zuìhòu		finally
17. 藍	lán	Adj	blue
18. 麻煩	máfan	Adj	troublesome
19. 還是	háishi	Conj	had better [See G4]
20. 出租汽車	chūzū qìchē		taxi
出租	chūzū	V	to rent out; to let
租	zū	V	to rent
21. 開車	kāi chē	VO	to drive a car
開	kāi	V	to drive; to operate
22. 送	sòng	V	to see off or out; to take someone (somewhere)

Dialogue: *Pinyin*

Wáng Péng:	Hánjià nǐ huí jiā ma?
Lǐ Yǒu:	Wǒ yào huí jiā.
Wáng Péng:	Fēijī piào nǐ mǎi le ma [G1]?
Lǐ Yǒu:	Yǐjīng mǎi le. Shì èrshíyī hào de.
Wáng Péng:	Fēijī shì jǐ diǎn de?
Lǐ Yǒu:	Wǎnshang bā diǎn de.
Wáng Péng:	Nǐ zěnme qù jīchǎng?
Lǐ Yǒu:	Wǒ xiǎng zuò gōnggòng qìchē huòzhě [G2] zuò dìtiě. Nǐ zhīdao zěnme zǒu ma?
Wáng Péng:	Nǐ xiān zuò yí hào [1] qìchē, zuò sān zhàn xià chē, ránhòu huàn dìtiě. Xiān zuò hóngxiàn, zài [G3] huàn lǜ xiàn, zuìhòu huàn lán xiàn.
Lǐ Yǒu:	Bù xíng, bù xíng, tài máfan le. Wǒ háishi [G4] zuò chūzū qìchē ba.
Wáng Péng:	Zuò chūzū qìchē tài guì, wǒ kěyǐ kāi chē sòng nǐ qù.
Lǐ Yǒu:	Xièxie nǐ.
Wáng Péng:	Bú yòng kèqi.

```
Li You                          *              Airport
Bus #1-------------⊘----------⊘----------⊘ ⊗ *              +
            Stop                *              +
                                * Red          + Blue
                                *              +
            Green               *              +
==========================  ⊗ ============= === ⊗ +
                                *              +
                                *              +
```

Dialogue: *Chinese*

王朋：寒假你回家嗎？

李友：我要回家。

王朋：<u>飛機票你買了嗎</u>^(G1)？

李友：已經買了。是二十一號的。

王朋：飛機是幾點的？

李友：晚上八點的。

王朋：你怎麼去機場？

李友：我想坐公共汽車<u>或者</u>^(G2)坐地鐵。你知道怎
　　　麼走嗎？

王朋：你先坐一號⁽¹⁾汽車，坐三站下車，然後換地
　　　鐵。<u>先</u>坐紅線，<u>再</u>^(G3)換綠線，最後換藍線。

李友：不行，不行，太麻煩了。我<u>還是</u>^(G4)坐出租
　　　汽車吧。

王朋：坐出租汽車太貴，我可以開車送你去。

李友：謝謝你。

王朋：不用客氣。

Notes:

(1) Both 號(hào) and 路(lù) are used to refer to bus routes. Therefore, 一路車
(yī lù chē) is also used to refer to Bus #1.

A LETTER: *THANKING SOMEONE FOR A RIDE*

Vocabulary

1.	不過	búguò	Conj	however; but
2.	讓	ràng	V	to allow or cause (somebody to do something)
3.	花	huā	V	to spend
4.	不好意思	bù hǎoyìsi	CE	to feel embarrassed
5.	這幾天	zhè jǐ tiān		the past few days
6.	每天	měitiān		every day
	每	měi	Prep	every; each (usually followed by a measure word)
7.	高速公路	gāosù gōnglù		super highway; highway
	高速	gāosù	Adj	high speed
	公路	gōnglù	N	highway; road
	路	lù	N	road
8.	緊張	jǐnzhāng	Adj	nervous
9.	自己	zìjǐ	Pr	oneself
10.	新年	xīnnián	N	new year
11.	快	kuài	Adv	soon; be about to; before long (usually takes 了 {le} at the end of the sentence)
12.	快樂	kuàilè	Adj	happy

A Letter: *Pinyin*

Wáng Péng:

Xièxie nǐ nà tiān kāi chē sòng wǒ dào jīchǎng. Búguò, ràng nǐ huā nàme duō shíjiān, zhēn bù hǎoyìsi. Wǒ zhè jǐ tiān <u>měi</u> tiān <u>dōu</u> ^(G5) kāi chē chūqu kàn lǎo péngyou. Zhèr de rén kāi chē kāi de hěn kuài. Wǒ zài gāosù gōnglù shang kāi chē, zhēn yǒu diǎn(r) jǐnzhāng. Kěshì zhèr méiyǒu gōnggòng qìchē, yě méiyǒu dìtiě, hěn bù fāngbiàn, zhǐ néng zìjǐ kāi chē.

Xīnnián kuài dào le, zhù nǐ xīnnián kuàilè!

Lǐ Yǒu

Shí'èryuè èrshíliù rì

A Letter: *Chinese*

王朋：

謝謝你那天開車送我到機場。不過，讓你花那麼多時間，真不好意思。我這幾天每天都^(G5)開車出去看老朋友。這兒的人開車開得很快。我在高速公路上開車，真有點兒緊張。可是這兒沒有公共汽車，也沒有地鐵，很不方便，只能自已開車。

新年快到了，祝你新年快樂！

李友

十二月二十六日

Supplementary Vocabulary

1.	走路	zǒulù	VO	walk
2.	火車	huǒchē	N	train
3.	計程車	jìchéngchē	N	taxi
4.	電車	diànchē	N	cable car; trolley bus; tram
5.	船	chuán	N	boat; ship
6.	輛	liàng	M	(a measure word for cars)

Review Dialogue I and put the above pictures in the correct sequence by using the numbers 1-4.

GRAMMAR

1. Topic-Comment Sentences

In a topic-comment sentence, the topic appears at the beginning of the sentence, whether it is the initiator or receiver of the action. By placing the topic at the beginning of a sentence, it is very clear what the focus of the sentence is.

(1) 飛機票你買了嗎？

Fēijīpiào nǐ mǎi le ma?

(Have you bought the plane ticket?)

(2) 你的襯衫我給你媽媽了。

Nǐ de chènshān wǒ gěi nǐ māma le.

(I have given your shirt to your mom.)

(3) 朋友我有很多，可是都不在這兒。

Péngyou wǒ yǒu hěn duō, kěshì dōu bú zài zhèr.

(I have a lot of friends, but none are here.)

(4) 功課，我喜歡在圖書館做。

Gōngkè, wǒ xǐhuan zài túshūguǎn zuò.

(When it comes to home work, I like to do it in the library.)

2. 或者 (huòzhě, or)

或者 (huòzhě, or) is not to be used in an interrogative sentence. It should not be confused with 還是 (háishi, or), which is used in the interrogative.

(1) A: 你今天晚上做什麼？

Nǐ jīntiān wǎnshang zuò shénme?

(What are you going to do tonight?)

B: 聽音樂或者看錄像。

Tīng yīnyuè huòzhě kàn lùxiàng.

(Listen to music or watch a video tape.)

(2) A: 你喜歡學中文還是喜歡學日文？

Nǐ xǐhuan xué Zhōngwén háishi xǐhuan xué Rìwén?

(Do you like studying Chinese or Japanese?)

B: 中文或者日文我都喜歡學。

Zhōngwén huòzhě Rìwén wǒ dōu xǐhuan xué.

(I like studying both Chinese and Japanese.)

(3) A: 你喜歡什麼顏色的鞋？黑的還是咖啡色的？

Nǐ xǐhuan shénme yánsè de xié? Hēi de háishi kāfēisè de?

(What color of shoes do you like, black or brown?)

B: 黑的或者咖啡色的我都不喜歡，我喜歡白的。

Hēi de huòzhě kāfēisè de wǒ dōu bù xǐhuan, wǒ xǐhuan bái de.

(I like neither black shoes nor brown shoes. I like white ones.)

(4) A: 你晚上看電影還是看電視？

Nǐ wǎnshang kàn diànyǐng háishi kàn diànshì?

(Are you going to see the movie or watch T.V. this evening?)

B: 看電影或者看電視都可以。

Kàn diànyǐng huòzhě kàn diànshì dōu kěyǐ.

(See a movie or watching T.V., either would be fine with me.)

(5) 明天你去開會或者他去開會都可以。

Míngtiān nǐ qù kāi huì huòzhě tā qù kāi huì dōu kěyǐ.

(Either you or he may attend tomorrow's meeting.)

In each of the (B) sentences and Sentence (5), 或者 cannot be replaced by 還是.

3. <u>先...再...</u> (xiān...zài..., first..., then...)

Sometimes 再 (zài, again) does not signify repetition. A sentence like "先看電影再吃飯" (Xiān kàn diànyǐng zài chī fàn. First go to the movie, then eat.) means "看電影以後吃飯" (Kàn diànyǐng yǐhòu zài chī fàn. Eat after seeing the movie.). More examples:

(1) A: 你什麼時候給媽媽打電話？

      Nǐ shénme shíhou gěi māma dǎ diànhuà?

      (When are you going to call Mom?)

  B: 下課以後再打。

      Xiàkè yǐhòu zài dǎ.

      (I'll call after class.)

(2) 我想先打球再去圖書館。

      Wǒ xiǎng xiān dǎqiú zài qù túshūguǎn.

      (I'd rather go to the library after playing ball.)

(3) 你先做功課再看電視。

      Nǐ xiān zuò gōngkè zài kàn diànshì.

      (You'd better finish doing the homework before you watch T.V.)

Note: The adverbs 先 and 再 should be placed before the verb, but never before the subject. Therefore, the following sentence is incorrect:

(3a) **Incorrect:** 先你做功課再你看電視。

      Xiān nǐ zuò gōngkè zài nǐ kàn diànshì.

4. <u>還是</u> (háishi, had better)

    還是 (háishi, had better) can be used to signify making a selection after pondering between two or more options. Sometimes in making such a decision one is forced to give up a preference.

(1) A: 高先生：下雨了。 怎麼辦？

      Gāo xiānsheng: Xià yǔ le. Zěnme bàn?

      (Mr. Gao: It's raining. What shall we do?)

  B: 白小姐： 我們還是在家看錄像吧。

      Bái xiǎojie: Wǒmen háishi zài jiā kàn lùxiàng ba.

      (Miss Bai: We had better stay home and watch a video.)

(2) A: 你說，明天看電影還是看打球？

　　Nǐ shuō, míngtiān kàn diànyǐng háishi kàn dǎ qiú?

　　(What do you think we should watch tomorrow, the movie or the ball game?)

B: 還是看電影吧。

　　Háishi kàn diànyǐng ba.

　　(Lets go to the movie.)

5. 每...都... (měi...dōu..., every)

In a sentence that contains the word 每(měi, every), usually 都 (dōu, all) has to be used after 每 (měi) and before the verb.

(1) 他每天晚上都看電視。

　　Tā měi tiān wǎnshang dōu kàn diànshì.

　　(He watches T.V. every evening.)

(2) 我每節課都來。

　　Wǒ měi jié kè dōu lái.

　　(I come for every class.)

(3) 這兒每個人我都認識。

　　Zhèr měi gè rén wǒ dōu rènshi.

　　(I know everyone here.)

(4) 王老師寫的字每個都好看。

　　Wáng lǎoshī xiě de zì měi gè dōu hǎokàn.

　　(Every character written by Teacher Wang looks nice.)

Can you name the three forms of transportation above?

PATTERN DRILLS

A. Topic-Comment Sentence

Example: (Wǒ yǒu hěn duō péngyou.)
     ---> Péngyou, wǒ yǒu hěn duō.

（我有很多朋友。）

---> 朋友，我有很多。

1. Wǒ bù cháng qù Xiǎo Bái jiā.
2. Tā dìdi bú huì xiě Zhōngwén xìn.
3. Wǒ yǐjīng mǎile diànnǎo.
4. Wǒ hěn xiǎng kàn nàge diànyǐng.
5. Tā chángcháng hē píjiǔ.
6. Wǒ mǎi fēijīpiào le.

1.我不常去小白家。

2.她弟弟不會寫中文信。

3.我已經買了電腦。

4.我很想看那個電影。

5.他常常喝啤酒。

6.我買飛機票了。

B. 或者 (huòzhě)

Example: (jīntiān wǎnshang, kàn diànshì/kàn diànyǐng)
     ---> Wǒ xiǎng jīntiān wǎnshang kàn diànshì huòzhě kàn diànyǐng.

（今天晚上   看電視/看電影）

---> 我想今天晚上看電視或者看電影。

1. míngtiān shàngwǔ	zhǎo Wáng lǎoshī/zhǎo Lǐ lǎoshī wèn wèntí
2. míngtiān xiàwǔ	qù dǎ qiú/qù tiào wǔ
3. jīntiān wǎnshang	chī Zhōngguófàn/chī Rìběnfàn
4. zhè xuéqí	xué Zhōngwén/xué Rìwén

5. kàn lùxiàng   xīngqíliù/xīngqítiān
6. qù Wáng lǎoshī jiā   zuò dìtiě/zuò gōnggòng qìchē
7. qù Táiwān   jīnnián/míngnián
8. qù Xiǎo Bái jiā   xiàwǔ sān diǎn/sì diǎn
9. zuò gōngkè   jīntiān xiàwǔ/wǎnshang

1. 明天上午   找王老師/找李老師問問題

2. 明天下午   去打球/去跳舞

3. 今天晚上   吃中國飯/吃日本飯

4. 這學期   學中文/學日文

5. 看錄像   星期六/星期天

6. 去王老師家   坐地鐵/坐公共汽車

7. 去台灣   今年/明年

8. 去小白家   下午三點/四點

9. 做功課   今天下午/晚上

C. 先...再... (xiān...zài...)

Example: (chī zǎofàn, qù túshūguǎn)
     ---> Wǒ xiān chī zǎofàn zài qù túshūguǎn.

(吃早飯　去圖書館)
--> 我先吃早飯，再去圖書館。

1.   qù túshūguǎn   shàng Zhōngwénkè
2.   shàng Zhōngwénkè   shàng diànnǎokè
3.   chī wǎnfàn   qù kàn diànyǐng
4.   zuò gōngkè   qù dǎ qiú
5.   liànxí fāyīn   xiě Hànzì
6.   hē píjiǔ   chī àn
7.   kàn lùxiàng   tiào wǔ
8.   tīng Měiguó yīnyuè   tīng Zhōngguó yīnyuè

1.	去圖書館	上中文課
2.	上中文課	上電腦課
3.	吃晚飯	去看電影
4.	做功課	去打球
5.	練習發音	寫漢字
6.	喝啤酒	吃飯
7.	看錄像	跳舞
8.	聽美國音樂	聽中國音樂

D. 還是 (háishi)

Example: (kàn hóngyè/kàn lùxiàng)
    ---> A: Wǒmen kàn hóngyè háishi kàn lùxiàng?
    ---> B: Wǒmen hàishi kàn lùxiàng ba.

(看紅葉/看錄像)

    -->A: 我們看紅葉還是看錄像？

    -->B: 我們還是看錄像吧。

1.	kàn diànyǐng	kàn diànshì
2.	xué Zhōngwén	xué Fǎwén
3.	qù Táiběi wánr	qù Shànghǎi wánr
4.	shàng Zhōngwénkè	shàng diànnǎokè
5.	xiān dǎ qiú	xiān zuò gōngkè
6.	qù chī Zhōngguófàn	qù chī Měiguófàn
7.	jīnnián qù Táiwān	míngnián qù Táiwān
8.	qù túshūguǎn zuò gōngkè	zài sùshè zuò gōngkè

1.	看電影	看電視
2.	學中文	學法文
3.	去台北玩兒	去上海玩兒
4.	上中文課	上電腦課

5.　先打球　　　　　　　　先做功課

6.　<u>去吃中國飯</u>　　　　　　去吃美國飯

7.　今年去台灣　　　　　　<u>明年去台灣</u>

8.　<u>去圖書館做功課</u>　　　　在宿舍做功課

E. 每...都... (měi...dōu...)

Example:　(wǎnshang, kàn diànshì)
　　　　---> Tā měitiān wǎnshang dōu kàn diànshì.

（晚上　　　　　看電視）

--> 他每天晚上都看電視。

1.	xiàwǔ	liànxí Zhōngwén
2.	zǎoshang	tīng Zhōngwén lùyīn
3.	zì	xiě de hěn hǎo
4.	yīfu	shì xīn de
5.	rén	rènshi
6.	wǎnshang	shí diǎnzhōng shuìjiào
7.	xīngqīliù	gěi māma dǎ diànhuà
8.	chènshān	shì báisè de
9.	shū	hěn yǒuyìsi

1.　下午　　　　練習中文

2.　早上　　　　聽中文錄音

3.　字　　　　　寫得很好

4.　衣服　　　　是新的

5.　人　　　　　認識

6.　晚上　　　　十點鐘睡覺

7.　星期六　　　給媽媽打電話

8.　襯衫　　　　是白色的

9.　書　　　　　很有意思

ENGLISH TEXT

Dialogue

Wang Peng:	Are you going home during the winter break?
Li You:	Yes, I am.
Wang Peng:	Have you booked the plane ticket?
Li You:	Yes. It's for the twenty-first.
Wang Peng:	When is the plane leaving?
Li You:	8 p.m.
Wang Peng:	How are you going to the airport?
Li You:	I'm thinking of taking the bus or the subway. Do you know how to get there?
Wang Peng:	You first take bus No. 1. Get off after three stops. Then take the subway. First take the red line, then change to the green line, and finally change to the blue line.
Li You:	Oh no, oh no. That's too much trouble. I'd better take a cab.
Wang Peng:	It's too expensive to take a cab. I can take you to the airport.
Li You:	Thank you very much.
Wang Peng:	Don't mention it.

A LETTER

December 26

Wang Peng:

Thank you for driving me to the airport the other day. It took you a lot of time. I feel really bad. The past few days I've been going out by car to see old friends. People here drive fast. I was really nervous driving on the highway. But there are no public buses or subway. It's very inconvenient. I have to drive.

New Year is almost here. Happy New Year!

Li You

TEXTS IN SIMPLIFIED CHARACTERS

Lesson One: Greetings
第一课　　问好

Dialogue I: *Chinese*

王先生[1]：你好[2]！

李小姐　：你好！

王先生　：请问，您贵姓[3]？

李小姐　：我姓[G1]李。你呢[G2]？

王先生　：我姓王，叫[G3]王朋。你叫什么名字[4]？

李小姐　：我叫李友。

Dialogue II: *Chinese*

李小姐：王先生，你是[G4]老师吗[G5]？

王先生：不[G6]，我不[1]是老师，我是学生。李
　　　　小姐，你呢？

李小姐：我也[G7]是学生。你是中国人吗？

王先生：是，我是中国人。你是美国人吗？

李小姐：我是美国人。

Lesson Two   Family
第二课　　家庭

Dialogue I: *Chinese*

(Wang Peng is in Little Gao's room pointing to a picture on the wall.)

王朋：小高[1]，那张[G1]照片是你的吗？

(They both walk toward the picture and then stand in front of it.)

小高：是。这是我爸爸，这是我妈妈。

王朋：这个男孩子是谁[G2]？

小高：他是我弟弟。

王朋：这个女孩子是你妹妹吗？

小高：不是，她是李先生的女儿。

王朋：李先生有[G3]儿子吗？

小高：他没有儿子。

Dialogue II: *Chinese*

李友：小张，你家有^(G4)几个⁽¹⁾人？

小张：我家有六个人。我爸爸、我妈妈⁽²⁾、一⁽³⁾个⁽⁴⁾哥哥、两^(G5)个姐姐和我。李小姐，你家有几个人？

李友：我家有五个人。爸爸、妈妈、两个妹妹和我。你爸爸妈妈做什么？

小张：我妈妈是英文老师，爸爸是律师，哥哥、姐姐都^(G6)是大学生。

李友：我妈妈也是老师，我爸爸是医生。

Lesson Three   Time
第三课   时间

Dialogue I: *Chinese*

(Little Gao is talking to Little Bai.)

小高：小白，九月十二^(G1)号^(G2)是星期几^(G2)？

小白：是星期四。

小高：那天是我的^(G3)生日。

小白：是吗？你今年多大⁽¹⁾？

小高：十八岁。

小白：星期四我请你吃晚饭^(G4)，怎么样？

小高：太好了。谢谢，谢谢⁽²⁾。

小白：你喜欢吃中国饭还是^(G5)美国饭？

小高：我是中国人，可是我喜欢吃美国饭。

小白：好，我们吃美国饭。

小高：星期四几点钟？

小白：七点半^(G2)怎么样？

小高：好，星期四晚上见。

小白：再见！

Dialogue II: *Chinese*

(Wang Peng and Little Bai are talking to each other.)

王朋 ： 小白，现在几点钟？

小白 ： 五点三刻。

王朋 ： 我六点一刻有事。

小白 ： 王朋，你明天忙不忙[G6]？

王朋 ： 我今天很忙，可是明天不忙。有事吗？

小白 ： 明天我请你吃晚饭，怎么样？

王朋 ： 为什么请我吃饭？

小白 ： 因为明天是小高的生日。

王朋 ： 是吗？好。还有[G7]谁？

小白 ： 还有我的同学小李。

王朋 ： 那太好了，我也认识小李。几点钟？

小白 ： 明天晚上七点半。

王朋 ： 好，明天七点半见。

Lesson Four   Hobbies
第四课   爱好

Dialogue I: *Chinese*

(Little Bai is talking to Little Gao.)

小白：小高，你周末喜欢做什么？

小高：我喜欢打球、看电视。你呢？

小白：我喜欢唱歌、跳舞，还喜欢听音乐。

小高：你也喜欢看书，对不对？

小白：对，有时候也喜欢看书。

小高：你<u>喜欢不喜欢</u>^(G1)看电影？

小白：喜欢。<u>我周末常常看电影</u>^(G2)。

小高：<u>那</u>^(G3)我们今天晚上<u>去看</u>^(G4)一个外国电影，
　　　怎么样？

小白：好。今天我请客。

小高：为什么你请客？

小白：因为昨天你请我吃饭，所以今天我请你看
　　　电影。

Dialogue II: *Chinese*

(Wang Peng is talking to Little Zhang.)

王朋：小张，好久不见，你好吗？

小张：我很好。你怎么样？

王朋：我也不错。这个周末你想^(G5)做什么？想不想去打球？

小张：打球？我不喜欢打球。

王朋：那我们去看电影，好吗^(G6)？

小张：看电影？我觉得看电影也没有意思。

王朋：那你喜欢做什么？

小张：我只喜欢吃饭、睡觉。

Lesson Five   Visiting Friends
第五课   看朋友

Dialogue: *Chinese*

小　高：谁呀？

王　朋：是我，王朋，还有李友。

小　高：请进，请进！李友，快进来！来，我介
　　　　绍<u>一下</u>^(G1)，这是我姐姐，高小音。

李　友：小音，您好。认识您很高兴⁽¹⁾。

高小音：认识你们我也很高兴。

李　友：你们家<u>很大</u>^(G2)，也很漂亮。

小　高：是吗？⁽²⁾。请坐，请坐。

王　朋：小音，你<u>在</u>^(G3)哪儿工作？

高小音：我在学校工作。你们想喝<u>点儿</u>^(G1)什么？
　　　　有茶、咖啡，还有啤酒。

王　朋：我喝啤<u>酒吧</u>^(G4)。

李　友：我不喝酒。我要一杯可乐，可以吗？

高小音：对不起，我们没有可乐。

李　友：那给我一杯水吧。

Narrative: *Chinese*

　　昨天晚上，王朋和李友去小高家玩儿。在小高家，他们认识了^(G5)小高的姐姐。她叫高小音，在学校的图书馆工作。小高请王朋喝啤酒，王朋喝了两瓶。李友不喝酒，只喝了一杯水。他们一起聊天儿、看电视。王朋和李友晚上十二点才^(G6)回家。

Lesson Six   Making Appointments
第六课   约时间

Dialogue I: *Chinese*

（李友给^(G1)老师打电话）

李　友：喂，请问王老师在吗？

王老师：我就是。您是哪位？

李　友：老师，您好。我是李友。

王老师：李友，你好，有事吗？

李　友：老师，今天下午您有时间吗？我想问您
　　　　几个问题。

王老师：对不起，今天下午我要^(G2)开会。

李　友：明天呢？

王老师：明天上午我有两节⁽¹⁾课，下午三点钟要
　　　　给二年级考试。

李　友：您什麽时候有空？

王老师：明天四点以后才有空。

李　友：要是您方便，四点半我到您的办公室
　　　　去，行吗？

王老师：四点半，没问题。我在办公室等你。

李　友：谢谢您。

王老师：不客气。

Dialogue II: *Chinese*

李友：喂，请问王朋在吗？

王朋：我就是。你是李友吧？有事吗？

李友：我想请你帮忙。

王朋：别^(G3)客气，有什么事？

李友：我下个星期要考中文⁽¹⁾，你帮我练习说中文，好吗？

王朋：好啊，但是你得^(G4)请我喝咖啡。

李友：喝咖啡，没问题。今天晚上你有空儿吗？

王朋：今天晚上有人请我吃饭，不知道⁽²⁾什么时候回来^(G5)。我回来以后给你打电话吧。

李友：好吧，我等你的电话。

Lesson Seven   Studying Chinese
第七课   学中文

Dialogue I: *Chinese*

（王朋跟李友说话）

王朋：李友，你上个星期考试考<u>得</u>^(G1)怎么样？

李友：考得不错，因为你帮助我复习，所以考得
不错。但是老师说我中国字写得<u>太</u>^(G2)慢！

王朋：是吗？以后我跟你一起练习写字，教你怎
么写，好不好？

李友：那太好了！我们现在<u>就</u>^(G3)写，给你笔。

王朋：好，我教你写"难"字。

李友：你写字写得很好，也很快。

王朋：哪里，哪里。你明天有中文课吗？

李友：有，明天我们学<u>第七</u>^(G4)课。

王朋：你预习了吗？

李友：预习了。第七课的语法很容易，我都懂，
可是生词太多，汉字也<u>有一点儿</u>^(G5)难。

王朋：今天晚上我跟你一起练习吧。

李友：好，谢谢你。

王朋：不谢，晚上见。

Dialogue II: *Chinese*

（李友跟小白说话）

李友：小白，你平常来得很早，今天<u>怎么</u>(G6)来得
        这么晚？

小白：我昨天预习中文，半夜一点<u>才</u>(G3)睡觉，你
        也睡得很晚吗？

李友：我昨天十点<u>就</u>(G3)睡了。因为王朋帮我练习
        中文，所以我功课做得很快。

小白：有个中国朋友<u>真</u>(G2)好。

（上中文课）

老师：大家早(1)，现在我们开始上课。<u>第七</u>(G4)课
        你们都预习了吗？

学生：预习了。

老师：李友，请你念课文。...你念得很好。你
        昨天晚上听录音了吧？

李友：我没听。

小白：但是她的朋友常常帮助(2)她。

老师：你的朋友是中国人吗？

李友：是的。

小白：他是一个男的，很帅(3)，叫王朋。

Lesson Eight   School Life
第八课   学校生活

A Diary: *Chinese*

李友的一篇日记

八月九日   星期一

我今天早上七点半起床(G1)，洗了澡以後就(G2)吃早饭。我一边吃饭，一边(G3)听录音。九点钟到教室去上课(G4)。

第一节课是中文，老师教我们发音(G5)、生词和语法，也教我们写字，还给了(G6)我们一篇新课文，这篇课文很有意思。第二节课是电脑课，很难。中午我和同学们一起到餐厅去吃午饭。我们一边吃，一边练习说中文。下午我到图书馆去看报。四点钟王朋来找我去打球。五点三刻吃晚饭。七点半我去小白的宿舍跟他聊天(儿)。到那儿的时候，他正在(G7)做功课。我八点半回家。睡觉以前，给王朋打了一个电话，告诉他明天要考试。他说他已经知道了。

A Letter: *Chinese*

一封信

张小姐：

　　你好！好久不见，最近怎么样？

　　这个学期我很忙，<u>除了</u>专业课<u>以外</u>，<u>还</u>(G8)得学中文。我们的中文课很有意思。因为我们的中文老师只<u>会</u>(G9)说中文，不会说英文，所以上课的时候我们只说中文，不说英文。开始我不习惯，後来，我有了一个中国朋友，他说话说得很清楚，常常跟我一起练习说中文，所以我的中文进步得很快。

　　你喜欢听音乐吗？下星期六，我们学校有一个音乐会，希望你<u>能</u>(G9)来。我用中文写信写得很不好，请别笑我。 祝

好

　　　　　　　　　　　　　　你的朋友
　　　　　　　　　　　　　　意文
　　　　　　　　　　　　　　八月十日

Lesson Nine　　Shopping
第九课　　　买东西

Dialogue I: *Chinese*

（买东西）

售货员：小姐[1]，<u>您要</u>[G1]买什么衣服？

李小姐：我想买一<u>件</u>[G2]衬衫。

售货员：您喜欢什么颜色<u>的</u>[G3]，黄的还是红的？

李小姐：我喜欢穿红的。我还想买一<u>条</u>[G2]裤子。

售货员：<u>多</u>[G4]大的？大号、中号还是小号的？

李小姐：中号的。不要太贵的，也不要太便宜[2]
　　　　的。

售货员：这条裤子和这件衬衫怎么样？

李小姐：很好，在哪儿付钱？

售货员：在这儿。

李小姐：一共多少钱？

售货员：衬衫二十<u>块</u>五，裤子三十二<u>块</u>九<u>毛</u>九，
　　　　一共是五十三<u>块</u>四<u>毛</u>九<u>分</u>[G5]。

李小姐：好，这是一百块钱。

售货员：找您四十六块五毛一。谢谢。

Dialogue II: *Chinese*

李小姐：对不起，这双鞋太小了。能不能换一
双？

售货员：没问题。您看，这双怎么样？

李小姐：也不行，这双跟那双<u>一样</u>^(G6)大。

售货员：那这双黑的呢？

李小姐：这双鞋<u>虽然</u>大小合适，<u>可是</u>^(G7)颜色不
好。有没有咖啡色的？

售货员：对不起，只有黑的。

李小姐：那好吧。我还要付钱吗？

售货员：不用，这双的钱跟那双一样。

Lesson Ten   Talking about the Weather
第十课   谈天气

Dialogue I: *Chinese*

谢小姐：今天天气比^(G1)昨天好，不下雨了^(G2)。

高先生：明天天气怎么样？希望明天也不下雨。

谢小姐：我看了报上的天气预报，明天天气比今
　　　　天更好。不但不会^(G3)下雨，而且会暖和
　　　　一点儿。

高先生：太好了！我约了李小姐明天去公园看红
　　　　叶。

谢小姐：是吗？可是李小姐今天早上跟王先生
　　　　去上海了。

高先生：真的啊？那我明天怎么办？

谢小姐：你在家看录像吧！

Dialogue II

小叶：真糟糕，又^(G4)下大雨了。

小夏：刚才我看报了，报上说，这个星期天气都不好，下个星期天气才会^(G3)好。

小叶：真的啊？那这个週末不能出去玩了。最近天气太热，真不舒服。

小夏：台北夏天的天气就是这样。两个月以后，天气就会比现在凉快一点儿了。

小叶：两个月以后？下个月我就回美国去了。

小夏：台湾春天常常下雨，冬天很冷，夏天又闷又热^(G5)。你下次最好秋天来。

Lesson Eleven   Transportation
第十一课   交通

Dialogue: *Chinese*

王朋：寒假你回家吗？

李友：我要回家。

王朋：<u>飞机票你买了吗</u>(G1)？

李友：已经买了。是二十一号的。

王朋：飞机是几点的？

李友：晚上八点的。

王朋：你怎么去机场？

李友：我想坐公共汽车<u>或者</u>(G2)坐地铁。你知道怎
　　　么走吗？

王朋：你先坐一号汽车，坐三站下车，然后换地
　　　铁。<u>先</u>坐红线，<u>再</u>(G3)换绿线，最后换蓝线。

李友：不行，不行，太麻烦了。我<u>还是</u>(G4)坐出租
　　　汽车吧。

王朋：坐出租汽车太贵，我可以开车送你去。

李友：谢谢你。

王朋：不用客气。

A Letter: *Chinese*

王朋：

　　谢谢你那天开车送我到机场。不过，让你花那麽多时间，真不好意思。我这几天每天都^(G5)开车出去看老朋友。这儿的人开车开得很快。我在高速公路上开车，真有点儿紧张。可是这儿没有公共汽车，也没有地铁，很不方便，只能自己开车。

　　新年快到了，祝你新年快乐！

　　　　　　　　　　　　李友

　　　　　　　　　　　十二月二十六日

中國地圖

Map of China

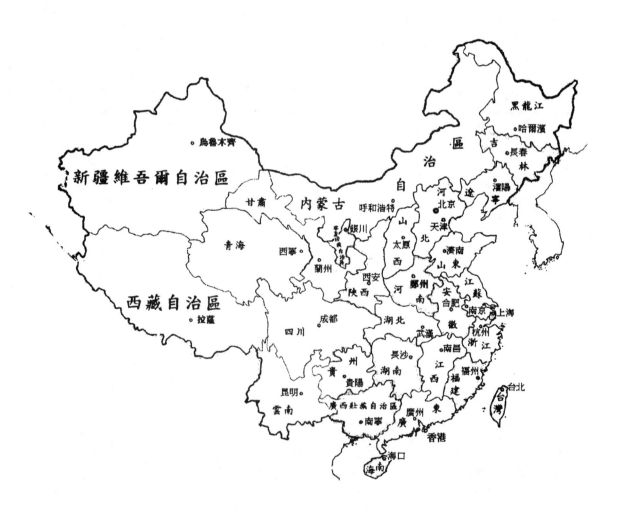

Appendix: Place Names in China

Names of provinces in China		Capital cities	
1. 安徽	Ānhuī	合肥	Héféi
2. 福建	Fújiàn	福州	Fúzhōu
3. 甘肅	Gānsù	蘭州	Lánzhōu
4. 廣東	Guǎngdōng	廣州	Guǎngzhōu
5. 貴州	Guìzhōu	貴陽	Guìyáng
6. 海南	Hǎinán	海口	Hǎikǒu
7. 河北	Héběi	石家莊	Shíjiāzhuāng
8. 河南	Hénán	鄭州	Zhèngzhōu
9. 黑龍江	Hēilóngjiāng	哈爾濱	Hā'ěrbīn
10. 湖北	Húběi	武漢	Wǔhàn
11. 湖南	Húnán	長沙	Chángshā
12. 吉林	Jílín	長春	Chángchūn
13. 江蘇	Jiāngsū	南京	Nánjīng
14. 江西	Jiāngxī	南昌	Nánchāng
15. 遼寧	Liáoníng	瀋陽	Shěnyáng
16. 青海	Qīnghǎi	西寧	Xīníng
17. 山東	Shāndōng	濟南	Jǐnán
18. 山西	Shānxī	太原	Tàiyuán
19. 陝西	Shǎnxī	西安	Xī'ān
20. 四川	Sìchuān	成都	Chéngdū
21. 雲南	Yúnnán	昆明	Kūnmíng
22. 浙江	Zhèjiāng	杭州	Hángzhōu
23. 台灣	Táiwān [See next page]		

Municipalities directly under the central government and the provinces that they are in.

1. 北京	Běijīng	河北	Héběi
2. 上海	Shànghǎi	江蘇	Jiāngsū
3. 天津	Tiānjīn	河北	Héběi
4. 重慶	Chóngqìng	四川	Sìchuān

Autonomous regions	Capital cities
1. 内蒙古自治區 Nèi Měnggǔ Zìzhìqū	呼和浩特 Hūhéhàotè (Huhhot)
2. 廣西壯族自治區 Guǎngxī Zhuàngzú Zìzhìqū	南寧 Nánníng
3. 寧夏回族自治區 Níngxià Huízú Zìzhìqū	銀川 Yínchuān
4. 新疆維吾爾自治區 Xīnjiāng Wéiwǔ'ěr (Uygur) Zìzhìqū	烏魯木齊 Wūlǔmùqí (Urumqi))
5. 西藏自治區 Xīzàng Zìzhìqū	拉薩 Lāsà (Lhasa)
6. 香港特別行政區 Xiānggǎng tèbié xíngzhèng qū	Hong Kong Special District Hong Kong *

Other major cities in China and the provinces that they are in.

1. 重慶	Chóngqìng	四川	Sìchuān
2. 青島	Qīngdǎo	山東	Shāndōng
3. 大連	Dàlián	遼寧	Liáoníng
4. 桂林	Guìlín	廣西壯族自治區 Guǎngxī Zhuàngzú Zìzhìqū	

Major cities in Taiwan**

1. 台北	Táiběi	Taipei
2. 高雄	Gāoxióng	Kaohsiung
3. 台中	Táizhōng	Taichung
4. 台南	Táinán	Tainan
5. 台東	Táidōng	Taitung
6. 花蓮	Huālián	Hualien

* Hong Kong rejoined China on July 1, 1997, after being a British colony for 99 years.

** Taiwan (the Republic of China) is not governed by China (the People's Republic of China). Both the governments in China (controlled by the Communist party) and Taiwan (controlled by the Nationalist Party) claimed that Taiwan is a province of China.

Vocabulary Index: Lessons 1-11

<u>A</u>

| a | 啊 | 啊 | P | (used to emphasize interrogation) | 6 |

<u>B</u>

bā	八	八	Nu	eight	Intro.
bàba	爸爸	爸爸	N	dad	2
ba	吧	吧	P	(used to soften the tone)	5
bái	白	白	Adj	(a surname); white	3
bǎi	百	百	Nu	hundred	9
bǎishìkělè	百事可樂	百事可乐	N	Pepsi	5x
bàn	半	半	Nu	half; half an hour	3
bànyè	半夜	半夜	T	midnight	7
bàngōngshì	辦公室	办公室	N	office	6
bāng	幫	帮	V	to help	6
bāng máng	幫忙	帮忙	VO	to help; to do someone a favor	6
bāngzhù	幫助	帮助	V	to help	7
bàngqiú	棒球	棒球	N	baseball	4x
bào	報	报	N	newspaper	8
bàoshang	報上	报上		in/on the newspaper	10
bēi	杯	杯	M	cup; glass	5
běnzi	本子	本子	N	notebook	7x
bǐ	筆	笔	N	pen	7
bǐ	比	比	Prep.	(indicates comparison)	10
biǎo	錶	表	N	watch	3x
bié	別	別		don't	6
bié (de)	別（的）	別（的）	Adv	other	4
bié kèqi	別客氣	別客气	CE	Don't be so polite!	6
bù	不	不	Adv	not; no	1
bú kèqi	不客氣	不客气	CE	You are welcome.	6
bú xiè	不謝	不谢	CE	don't mention it; not at all	7
bú yòng	不用	不用	CE	need not	9
búcuò	不錯	不错	Adj	not bad; pretty good	4
búdàn..., érqiě	不但…而且	不但...而且	Conj	not only..., but also	10
búguò	不過	不过	Conj	however; but	11
bù hǎoyìsi	不好意思	不好意思	CE	to feel embarrassed	11

<u>C</u>

cái	才	才	Adv	not until	5
cāntīng	餐廳	餐厅	N	dining room	8
chá	茶	茶	N	tea	5
chà	差	差	V	to be short of; lack	3x
cháng	長	长	Adj	long	9x
chángcháng	常常	常常	Adv	often	4
chàng	唱	唱	V	to sing	4
chàng gē	唱歌	唱歌	VO	to sing (a song)	4
cháoshī	潮濕	潮湿	Adj	wet; humid	10x

chē	車	车	N	vehicle; car	11
chēzhàn	車站	车站	N	(of bus, train, etc.) stop; station	11
chènshān	襯衫	衬衫	N	shirt	9
chī	吃	吃	V	to eat	3
chī fàn	吃飯	吃饭	VO	to eat (a meal)	3
chūqu	出去	出去	VP	to go out	10
chūzū	出租	出租	V	to rent out; to let	11
chūzū qìchē	出租汽車	出租汽车	N	taxi	11
chúle...yǐwài	除了...以外	除了...以外	Conj	in addition to; besides	8
chūntiān	春天	春天	N	spring	10
chuān	穿	穿	V	to wear	9
chuán	船	船	N	boat; ship	11x
chuáng	床	床	N	bed	8
cì	次	次	M	(a measure word for occurrence)	10
cuò	錯	错	Adj	wrong	4

D

dǎ	打	打	V	to hit; to strike	4
dǎ diànhuà	打電話	打电话	VO	to make a phone call	6
dǎ gōng	打工	打工	VO	to have a part-time job	5x
dǎ qiú	打球	打球	VO	to play ball	4
dà	大	大	Adj	big; old	3
dàjiā	大家	大家	Pr	everybody	7
dàxiǎo	大小	大小	N	size	9
dàxué	大學	大学	N	university; college	2
dàxuéshēng	大學生	大学生	N	college student	2
dàyī	大衣	大衣	N	overcoat	9x
dài	戴	戴	V	to wear (hat, glasses, etc.)	9x
dànshì	但是	但是	Conj	but	6
dào	到	到	V	to arrive	8
dào...qù	到...去	到...去		to go to (a place)	6
de	的	的		(indicating a possessive)	2
de shíhou	的時候	的时候		when...; at the time of...	8
de	得	得	P	(a particle)	7
Déguó	德國	德国	PN	Germany	1x
Déguórén	德國人	德国人	N	German people/person	1x
Déwén	德文	德文	N	German	6x
děi	得	得	AV	must; have to	6
děng	等	等	V	to wait	6
dì	第	第	prefix	(prefix for ordinal numbers)	7
dìdi	弟弟	弟弟	N	younger brother	2
dìtiě	地鐵	地铁	N	subway	11
diǎn	點	点	N	o'clock	3
diǎn(r)	點(兒)	点(儿)	M	a little; a bit; some	5
diǎnzhōng	點鐘	点钟	N	o'clock	3
diàn	電	电	N	electricity	4
diànchē	電車	电车	N	cable car; trolley bus; tram	11x
diànhuà	電話	电话	N	telephone	6
diànnǎo	電腦	电脑	N	computer	8

diànshì	電視	电视	N	TV	4
diànyǐng	電影	电影	N	movie	4
dǐng	頂	顶	M	(a measure word for hat)	9x
dōngtiān	冬天	冬天	N	winter	10
dōngxi	東西	东西	N	things; object	9
dǒng	懂	懂	V	to understand	7
dōu	都	都	Adv	both; all	2
duǎn	短	短	Adj	short	9x
duì	對	对	Adj.	right; correct	4
duì bu qǐ	對不起	对不起	CE	I'm sorry.	5
duì le	對了	对了	CE	That's right!	4x
duō	多	多	Adv	(inquiry about degree)	3
duō	多	多	Adj	many; much	7
duō dà	多大	多大	CE	how old	3
duōshao	多少	多少	QW	how much; how many	9

E

Éguó	俄國	俄国	PN	Russia	6x
Éwén	俄文	俄文	N	Russian	6x
érzi	兒子	儿子	N	son	2
èr	二	二	Nu	two	Intro.

F

fāyīn	發音	发音	N	pronunciation	8
Fǎguó	法國	法国	PN	France	1x
Fǎguórén	法國人	法国人	N	French people/person	1x
Fǎwén	法文	法文	N	French	6x
fàn	飯	饭	N	meal; (cooked) rice	3
fāngbiàn	方便	方便	Adj	convenient	6
fēi	飛	飞	V	to fly	11
fēijī	飛機	飞机	N	airplane	11
fēijīchǎng	飛機場	飞机场	N	airport	11
Fēilǜbīn	菲律賓	菲律宾	PN	the Philippines	6x
fēn	分	分	M	cent	9
fēn	分	分	N	minute	3x
fěnhóngsè	粉紅色	粉红色	Adj	pink	9x
fēng	封	封	M	(a measure word for letters)	8
fù qián	付錢	付钱	VO	to pay money	9
fùxí	復習	复习	V	to review	7

G

gǎnlǎnqiú	橄欖球	橄榄球	N	football	4x
gāngbǐ	鋼筆	钢笔	N	fountain pen	7x
gāngcái	剛才	刚才	T	just now; a short moment ago	10
gāo	高	高		(a surname); tall	2
gāosù	高速	高速	Adj	high speed	11
gāosù gōnglù	高速公路	高速公路	N	super highway; highway	11
gāoxìng	高興	高兴	Adj	happy; pleased	5
gàosu	告訴	告诉	V	to tell	8

gē	歌	歌	N	song	4
gēge	哥哥	哥哥	N	older brother	2
gè	個	个	M	(the general measure word)	2
gěi	給	给	V	to give	5
gěi	給	给	Prep	to; for	6
gēn	跟	跟	Conj	and	7
gèng	更	更	Adv	even more	10
gōnggòng	公共	公共	Adj	public	11
gōnggòng qìchē	公共汽車	公共汽车	N	bus	11
gōngkè	功課	功课	N	schoolwork; homework	7
gōnglù	公路	公路	N	highway; road	11
gōngyuán	公園	公园	N	park	10
gōngzuò	工作	工作	V	to work	5
guì	貴	贵	Adj	expensive	9
guì	貴	贵	Adj	honorable	1
guì xìng	貴姓	贵姓	CE	What is your honorable surname?	1

<u>H</u>

háishi	還是	还是	Conj	or	3
háishi	還是	还是	Conj	had better	11
háiyǒu	還有	还有	Adv	also; in addition	3
háizi	孩子	孩子	N	child	2
Hánguó	韓國	韩国	PN	Korea	6x
Hánwén	韓文	韩文	N	Korean	6x
hánjià	寒假	寒假	N	winter vacation	11
Hànzì	漢字	汉字	N	Chinese characters	7
hǎo	好	好	Adj	fine; good; nice; O.K.	1
hǎo	好	好	Adj	O.K.	3
hǎochī	好吃	好吃	Adj	good to eat; delicious	5x
hǎohē	好喝	好喝	Adj	good to drink; tasty	5x
hǎojiǔ	好久	好久	CE	a long time	4
hǎokàn	好看	好看	Adj	good-looking	5x
hǎowán(r)	好玩（兒）	好玩（儿）	Adj	fun	5x
hào	號	号	N	day of the month; number	3
hào	號	号	N	number; size	9
hē	喝	喝	V	to drink	5
hé	和	和	Conj	and	2
héshì	合適	合适	Adj	suitable	9
hēi	黑	黑	Adj	black	9
hěn	很	很	Adv	very	3
hóng	紅	红	Adj	red	9
hóngyè	紅葉	红叶	N	red autumn leaves	10
hòulái	後來	后来	T	later	8
hòunián	後年	后年	T	the year after next	3x
hòutiān	後天	后天	T	the day after tomorrow	3x
huā	花	花	V	to spend	11
huà	話	话	N	speech; talk; words	6
huàn	換	换	V	to change; to exchange	9
huáng	黃（黄）	黄（黄）	Adj	yellow	9

huī	灰	灰	Adj	grey	9x
huí	回	回	V	to return	5
huí jiā	回家	回家	VO	to go home	5
huílai	回來	回来	VC	to come back	6
huì	會	会	AV	can; know how to	8
huì	會	会	AV	(indicates probability)	10
huǒchē	火車	火车	N	train	11x
huòzhě	或者	或者	Conj	or	11

J

jī	機	机	N	machine	11
jīchǎng	機場	机场	N	airport	11
jǐ	幾	几	QW	how many	2
jǐ	幾	几	Nu	several	6
jìchéngchē	計程車	计程车	N	taxi	11x
jiā	家	家	N	family; home	2
Jiānádà	加拿大	加拿大	PN	Canada	10x
jiákè	夾克	夹克	N	jacket	9x
jiàn	見	见	V	to see	3
jiàn	件	件	M	(a measure word for shirts, etc.)	9
jiào	叫	叫	V	to be called	1
jiāo	教	教	V	to teach	7
jiàoshì	教室	教室	N	classroom	8
jié	節	节	M	(a measure word for classes)	6
jiějie	姐姐	姐姐	N	older sister	2
jièshào	介紹	介绍	V	to introduce	5
jīnnián	今年	今年	T	this year	3
jīntiān	今天	今天	T	today	3
jǐnzhāng	緊張	紧张	Adj	nervous	11
jìn	近	近	Adj	near	8
jìn	進	进	V	to enter	5
jìnbù	進步	进步	V	to make progress	8
jìnlai	進來	进来	VC	come in	5
jiǔ	九	九	Nu	nine	Intro.
jiǔ	久	久	Adj	a long time	4
jiǔ	酒	酒	N	wine	5
jiǔyuè	九月	九月	N	September	3
jiù	就	就	Adv	(indicating verification)	6
jiù	就	就	Adv	(indicating sooner than expected)	7
júhóngsè	橘紅色	橘红色	Adj	orange	9x
juéde	覺得	觉得	V	to feel	4

K

kāfēi	咖啡	咖啡	N	coffee	5
kāfēisè	咖啡色	咖啡色	N	coffee color; brown	9
kāi	開	开	V	to hold (a meeting, party, etc.)	6
kāi	開	开	V	to drive; to operate	11
kāi chē	開車	开车	VO	to drive a car	11
kāi huì	開會	开会	VO	to have a meeting	6

kāishǐ	開始	开始	V	to start	7
kāishǐ	開始	开始	N/V	in the beginning; to begin; to start	8
kàn	看	看	V	to watch; to look	4
kàn shū	看書	看书	VO	read books; read	4
kǎo	考	考	V	to give or take a test	6
kǎoshì	考試	考试	V/N	to give or take a test; test	6
kěkǒukělè	可口可樂	可口可乐	N	Coke	5x
kělè	可樂	可乐	N	cola	5
kěshì	可是	可是	Conj	but	3
kěyǐ	可以	可以	AV	can, may	5
kè	課	课	N	class; lesson	6
kèwén	課文	课文	N	text	7
kè	刻	刻	T	quarter (hour); 15 minutes	3
kèqi	客氣	客气	Adj	polite	6
kòng(r)	空(兒)	空(儿)	N	free time	6
kùzi	褲子	裤子	N	pants	9
kuài	塊	块	M	dollar	9
kuài	快	快	Adv	fast; quickly	5
kuài	快	快	Adj	quick; fast	7
kuài	快	快	Adv	soon; be about to; before long	11
kuàilè	快樂	快乐	Adj	happy	11
kuàngquánshuǐ	礦泉水	矿泉水	N	mineral water	5x

L

Lādīngwén	拉丁文	拉丁文	N	Latin	6x
lái	來	来	V	to come	5
lán	藍	蓝	Adj	blue	9x
lán	藍	蓝	Adj	blue	11
lánqiú	籃球	篮球	N	basketball	4x
lǎoshī	老師	老师	N	teacher	1
le	了	了	P	(indicating superlative degree)	3
lěng	冷	冷	Adj	cold	10
lǐ	李	李	N	(a surname); plum	1
Lǐ Yǒu	李友	李友	PN	(a person's name)	1
liángkuai	涼快	凉快	Adj	nice and cool (weather)	10
liǎng	兩	两	Nu	two; a couple of	2
liàng	輛	辆	M	(a measure word for cars)	11x
liànxí	練習	练习	V	to practice	6
liáo tiān(r)	聊天(兒)	聊天(儿)	VO	to chat	5
liù	六	六	Nu	six	Intro.
lù	路	路	N	road	11
lùxiàng	錄像	录像	N	video recording	10
lùyīn	錄音	录音	N	sound recording	7
lǜ	綠	绿	Adj	green	9x
lǜ	綠	绿	Adj	green	11
lǜshī	律師	律师	N	lawyer	2

M

| māma | 媽媽 | 妈妈 | N | mom | 2 |

máfan	麻煩	麻烦	Adj	troublesome	11
Mǎláixīyà	馬來西亞	马来西亚	PN	Malaysia	6x
ma	嗎	吗	QP	(a particle)	1
mǎi	買	买	V	to buy	9
mài	賣	卖	V	to sell	9x
màn	慢	慢	Adj	slow	7
máng	忙	忙	Adj	busy	3
máo	毛	毛	M	dime	9
máobǐ	毛筆	毛笔	N	writing brush	7x
máoyī	毛衣	毛衣	N	sweater	9x
màozi	帽子	帽子	N	hat	9x
méi	沒	没	Adv	not	2
méi wèntí	沒問題	没问题	CE	no problem	6
měi	每	每	Prep	every; each	11
měitiān	每天	每天	T	every day	11
Měiguó	美國	美国	PN	the United States of America	1
Měiguórén	美國人	美国人	N	American people/person	1
mèimei	妹妹	妹妹	N	younger sister	2
mēn	悶	闷	Adj	stuffy	10
míngnián	明年	明年	T	next year	3x
míngtiān	明天	明天	T	tomorrow	3
míngzi	名字	名字	N	name	1

<u>N</u>

nǎ/něi	哪	哪	QPr	which	6
nǎli	哪裏	哪里	CE	You flatter me; not at all.	7
nǎr	哪兒	哪儿	QPr	where	5
nà/nèi	那	那	Pr	that	2
nà	那	那	Conj	in that case; then	4
nàr	那兒	那儿	Pr	there	8
nán	男	男	N	male	2
nán de	男的	男的		male	7
nánháizi	男孩子	男孩子	N	boy	2
nán	難	难	Adj	difficult	7
nǎo	腦	脑	N	brain	8
ne	呢	呢	QP	(a particle)	1
néng	能	能	AV	can, able to	8
nǐ	你	你	Pr	you	1
nǐ hǎo	你好	你好	CE	How do you do? Hello!	1
nián	年	年	N	year	3
niánjí	年級	年级	N	grade in school	6
niàn	念	念	V	to read	7
nín	您	您	Pr	you (polite)	1
nuǎnhuo	暖和	暖和	Adj	warm (weather)	10
nǚ	女	女	N	female	2
nǚ'ér	女兒	女儿	N	daughter	2
nǚháizi	女孩子	女孩子	N	girl	2

P

páiqiú	排球	排球	N	volleyball	4x
péngyou	朋友	朋友	N	friend	1x
péngyou	朋友	朋友	N	friend	7
piān	篇	篇	M	(a measure word for essays, etc.)	8
piányi	便宜	便宜	Adj	cheap; inexpensive	9
piào	票	票	N	ticket	11
piàoliang	漂亮	漂亮	Adj	pretty	5
píjiǔ	啤酒	啤酒	N	beer	5
píng	瓶	瓶	M	bottle	5
píngcháng	平常	平常	T	usually	7
				place sooner than expected)	7
Pútáoyá	葡萄牙	葡萄牙	PN	Portugal	6x
Pútáoyáwén	葡萄牙文	葡萄牙文	N	Portuguese	6x

Q

qī	七	七	Nu	seven	Intro.
qǐ chuáng	起床	起床	VO	to get up	8
qìchē	汽車	汽车	N	automobile	11
qìshuǐ(r)	汽水(兒)	汽水(儿)	N	soft drink; soda pop	5x
qiānbǐ	鉛筆	铅笔	N	pencil	7x
qián	錢	钱	N	money	9
qiánnián	前年	前年	T	the year before last	3x
qiántiān	前天	前天	T	the day before yesterday	3x
qīngchu	清楚	清楚	Adj	clear	8
qíng	晴	晴	Adj	sunny; clear	10x
qǐng	請	请	V	please (polite form of request)	1
qǐng	請	请	V	to treat (somebody); to invite	3
qǐng wèn	請問	请问	CE	May I ask...	1
qǐng kè	請客	请客	VO	to invite someone to dinner; to play the host	4
qiūtiān	秋天	秋天	N	autumn; fall	10
qiú	球	球	N	ball	4
qúnzi	裙子	裙子	N	skirt	9x
qù	去	去	V	to go	4
qùnián	去年	去年	T	last year	3x

R

ránhòu	然後	然后	Adv	then	11
ràng	讓	让	V	to let; to make	11
rè	熱	热	Adj	hot	10
rén	人	人	N	people; person	1
rènshi	認識	认识	V	to know (someone);	3
rì	日	日	N	day; sun	3
Rìběn	日本	日本	PN	Japan	1x
Rìběnrén	日本人	日本人	N	Japanese people/person	1x
rìjì	日記	日记	N	diary	8
Rìwén	日文	日文	N	Japanese	6x
róngyì	容易	容易	Adj	easy	7

tiānqì	天氣	天气	N	weather	10
tiáo	條	条	M	(a measure word for long, objects)	9
tiào	跳	跳	V	to jump	4
tiào wǔ	跳舞	跳舞	VO	to dance	4
tīng	聽	听	V	to listen	4
tóngxué	同學	同学	N	classmate	3
túshūguǎn	圖書館	图书馆	N	library	5

W

wàzi	襪子	袜子	N	socks	9x
wàiguó	外國	外国	N	foreign country	4
wàitào	外套	外套	N	coat; jacket	9x
wán(r)	玩(兒)	玩(儿)	V	to have fun; to play	5
wǎn	晚	晚	N/Adj	evening; night; late	3
wǎnshang	晚上	晚上	T	evening; night	3
wǎnfàn	晚飯	晚饭	N	dinner; supper	3
wáng	王	王	N	(a surname); king	1
Wáng Péng	王朋	王朋	PN	(a person's name)	1
wǎngqiú	網球	网球	N	tennis	4x
wèi	為(爲)**	为(为)**	Prep	for	3
wèi	喂	喂	Interj	Hello!; Hey!	6
wèi	位	位	M	(a polite measure word for people)	6
wèishénme	為什麼	为什么	QPr	why	3
Wēngēhuá	溫哥華	温哥华	PN	Vancouver	10x
wén	文	文		language; written language	6
wèn	問	问	V	to ask	1
wèntí	問題	问题	N	question; problem	6
wǒ	我	我	Pr	I; me	1
wǒmen	我們	我们	Pr	we	3
wǔ	五	五	Nu	five	Intro.
wǔ	舞	舞	N	dance	4
wǔfàn	午飯	午饭	N	lunch	8
wǔjiào	午覺	午觉	N	nap	7x

X

Xīlà	希臘	希腊	PN	Greece	6x
Xīlàwén	希臘文	希腊文	N	Greek	6x
xīwàng	希望	希望	V	to hope	8
Xībānyá	西班牙	西班牙	PN	Spain	6x
Xībānyáwén	西班牙文	西班牙文	N	Spanish	6x
xīzhuāng	西裝	西装	N	a suit	9x
xíguàn	習慣	习惯	V	to be accustomed to	8
xǐhuan	喜歡	喜欢	V	to like; to prefer	3
xǐ zǎo	洗澡	洗澡	VO	to take a bath/shower	8
xià	下	下		next; under	6
xià chē	下車	下车	VO	to get off (a bus, train, etc.)	11
xià cì	下次	下次		next time	10
xiàge xīngqī	下個星期	下个星期	T	next week	6
xià(ge)yuè	下(個)月	下(个)月	T	next month	3x